POPULATION ECOLOGY

POPULATION ECOLOGY

By

Dr. Anupam Pandey

M.A., Ph.D., (Geography)

D.T.S., D.C.W.H

DISCOVERY PUBLISHING HOUSE PVT. LTD.

NEW DELHI-110 002

Published by:
Tilak Wasan
DISCOVERY PUBLISHING HOUSE PVT. LTD.
4383/4A, Ansari Road, Darya Ganj
New Delhi-110 002 (India)
Phone : +91-11-23279245, 43596064-65
Fax : +91-11-23253475
E-mail : parul.wasan@gmail.com
discoverypublishinghouse@gmail.com
web : www.discoverypublishinggroup.com

First Edition: **2012**

ISBN: 978-93-5056-113-3

Population Ecology

Printed at:
Shree Balaji Art Press
Delhi

Preface

Population ecology is a major sub-field of ecology that deals with the dynamics of species populations and how these populations interact with the environment.

The first journal publication of the Society of Population Ecology, titled *Population Ecology* (originally called Researches on Population Ecology), was released in 1952. Population ecology is concerned with the study of groups of organisms that live together in time and space. One of the first laws of population ecology is the Thomas Malthus' exponential law of population growth. This law states that:

> "...a population will grow (or decline) exponentially as long as the environment experienced by all individuals in the population remains constant".

An important concept in population ecology is the *r*/*K* selection theory. The first variable is *r* (the intrinsic rate of natural increase in population size, density independent) and the second variable is *K* (the carrying capacity of a population, density dependent). An *r*-selected species (e.g., many kinds of insects, such as aphids is one that has high rates of fecundity, low levels of parental investment in the young, and high rates of mortality before individuals reach maturity. Evolution favours productivity in *r*-selected species. In contrast, a *K*-selected species (such as humans) has low rates of fecundity, high levels of parental investment in the young, and low rates of mortality as individuals mature. Evolution in *K*-selected species favours efficiency in the conversion of more resources into fewer offspring.

Populations are also studied and conceptualized through the 'metapopulation' concept. The metapopulation concept was introduced in 1969:

> "as a population of populations which go extinct locally and recolonize".

Metapopulation ecology is a simplified model of the landscape into patches of varying levels of quality. Patches are either occupied or they are not. Migrants moving among the patches are structured into metapopulations either as sources or sinks. Source patches are productive sites that generate a seasonal supply of migrants to other patch locations. Sink patches are unproductive sites that only receive migrants. In metapopulation terminology there are emigrants (individuals that leave a patch) and immigrants (individuals that move into a patch). Metapopulation models examine patch dynamics over time to answer questions about spatial and demographic ecology. An important concept in metapopulation ecology is the rescue effect, where small patches of lower quality (i.e., sinks) are maintained by a seasonal influx of new immigrants. Metapopulation structure evolves from year to year, where some patches are sinks, such as dry years, and become sources when conditions are more favourable. Ecologists utilize a mixture of computer models and field studies to explain metapopulation structure.

The development of the field of population ecology owes much to the science of demography and the use of actuarial life tables. Population ecology has also played an important role in the development of the field of conservation biology, especially in the development of population viability analysis (PVA) which makes it possible to predict the long-term probability of a species persisting in a given habitat patch (*e.g.*, a national park).

While essentially a subfield of biology, population ecology provides many interesting problems for mathematicians and statisticians, who work mainly in the study of population dynamics.

Author

Contents

Introduction

Population ecology is a major sub-field of ecology that deals with the dynamics of species populations and how these populations interact with the environment.

The first journal publication of the Society of Population Ecology, titled *Population Ecology* (originally called Researches on Population Ecology), was released in 1952. Population ecology is concerned with the study of groups of organisms that live together in time and space. One of the first laws of population ecology is the Thomas Malthus' exponential law of population growth. This law states that:

> "...a population will grow (or decline) exponentially as long as the environment experienced by all individuals in the population remains constant".

This premise in population ecology provides the basis for formulating predictive theories and tests that follow. Simplified population models usually start with four key variables including death, birth, immigration, and emigration. Mathematical models used to calculate changes in population demographics and evolution hold the assumption (or null hypothesis) of no external influence. Models can be more mathematically complex where ". . . several competing hypotheses are simultaneously confronted with the data". For example, in a closed system where immigration and emigration does not take place, the per capita rates of change in a population can be described as:

$$dN / dT = B - D = bN - dN = (b - d)N = rN,$$

where N is the total number of individuals in the population, B is the number of births, D is the number of deaths, b and d are the per capita rates of birth and death respectively, and r is the per capita rate of population change. This formula can be read as the rate of change in the population (dN/dT) is equal to births minus deaths ($B - D$).

Using these techniques, Malthus' population principle of growth was later transformed into a mathematical model known as the logistic equation:

$$dN/dT = aN(1 - N/K),$$

where N is the biomass density, a is the maximum per-capita rate of change, and K is the carrying capacity of the population. The formula can be read as follows: the rate of change in the population (dN/dT) is equal to growth (aN) that is limited by carrying capacity ($1-N/K$). From these basic mathematical principles the discipline of population ecology expands into a field of investigation that queries the demographics of real populations and tests these results against the statistical models. The field of population ecology often uses data on life history and matrix algebra to develop projection matrices on fecundity and survivourship. This information is used for managing wildlife stocks and setting harvest quotas.

An important concept in population ecology is the r/K selection theory. The first variable is r (the intrinsic rate of natural increase in population size, density independent) and the second variable is K (the carrying capacity of a population, density dependent). An r-selected species (e.g., many kinds of insects, such as aphids is one that has high rates of fecundity, low levels of parental investment in the young, and high rates of mortality before individuals reach maturity. Evolution favours productivity in r-selected species. In contrast, a K-selected species (such as humans) has low rates of fecundity, high levels of parental investment in the young, and low rates of mortality as individuals mature. Evolution in K-selected species favors efficiency in the conversion of more resources into fewer offspring.

Populations are also studied and conceptualized through the 'metapopulation' concept. The metapopulation concept was introduced in 1969:

"as a population of populations which go extinct locally and recolonize".

Metapopulation ecology is a simplified model of the landscape into patches of varying levels of quality. Patches are either occupied or they are not. Migrants moving among the patches are structured into metapopulations either as sources or sinks. Source patches are productive sites that generate a seasonal supply of migrants to other patch locations. Sink patches are unproductive sites that only receive migrants. In metapopulation terminology there are emigrants (individuals that leave a patch) and immigrants (individuals that move into a patch). Metapopulation models examine patch dynamics over time to answer questions about spatial and demographic ecology. An important concept in metapopulation ecology is the rescue effect, where small patches of lower quality (i.e., sinks) are maintained by a seasonal influx of new immigrants. Metapopulation structure evolves from year to year, where some patches are sinks, such as dry years, and become sources when conditions are more favourable. Ecologists utilize a mixture of computer models and field studies to explain metapopulation structure.

The older term, autecology (from Greek: , *auto*, 'self'; , oikos, 'household'; and , logos, 'knowledge'), refers to roughly the same field of study, coming from the division of ecology into autecology—the study of individual species in relation to the environment — and synecology — the study of groups of organisms in relation to the environment — or community ecology. Odum considered that synecology should be divided into population ecology, community ecology, and ecosystem ecology, defining autecology as essentially 'species ecology'. However, for some time biologists have recognized that the more significant level of organization of a species is a population, because at this level the species gene pool is most coherent. In fact, Odum regarded 'autecology' as no longer a 'present tendency' in ecology (i.e., an archaic term), although included 'species ecology' — studies emphasizing life history and behaviour as adaptations to the environment of individual organisms or species — as one of four subdivisions of ecology.

The development of the field of population ecology owes much to the science of demography and the use of actuarial life tables. Population ecology has also played an important role in the development of the field of conservation biology, especially in the development of population viability analysis (PVA) which makes it possible to predict the long-term probability of a species persisting in a given habitat patch (*e.g.*, a national park).

While essentially a subfield of biology, population ecology provides many interesting problems for mathematicians and statisticians, who work mainly in the study of population dynamics.

Ecology

Ecology (from Greek: , 'house' or 'living relations'; a, 'study of') is the scientific study of the relation of living organisms to each other and their surroundings. Ecology includes the study of plant and animal populations, plant and animal communities and ecosystems. Ecologists study a range of living phenomena from the role of bacteria in nutrient recycling to the effects of tropical rain forest on the Earth's atmosphere.

The word 'ecology' ('oekologie') was first used by the German scientist Ernst Haeckel 1834-1919. Haeckel was a zoologist, artist, writer, and later in life a professor of comparative anatomy.

Ecology is a sub-discipline of biology, which is the study of life, branching out from the natural sciences in the late 19th century. Ecology is not synonymous with environment, environmentalism, natural history or environmental science. Ecology is closely related to the biological disciplines of physiology, evolution, genetics and behaviour.

Ecology seeks to explain:

- life processes and adaptations;
- distribution and abundance of organisms;
- the movement of materials and energy through living communities;
- the successional development of ecosystems; and
- the abundance and distribution of biodiversity in context of the environment.

There are many practical applications of ecology in conservation biology, wetland management, natural resource management (agriculture, forestry, fisheries), city planning (urban ecology), community health, economics, basic and applied science and it provides a conceptual framework for understanding and researching human social interaction (human ecology).

Scale and Complexity

Ecosystems regenerate after a disturbance such as fire, forming mosaics of different age groups structured across a landscape. Different seral stages in forested ecosystems starting from pioneers colonizing a disturbed site and maturing in successional stages leading to old-growth forests.

The processes that influence ecological phenomena vary through space and time. It can take thousands of years for ecological processes to mature; the life-span of a tree, for example, can encompass different successional stages. The ecological process is extended even further through time as trees die, decay and provide habitat as nurse logs or coarse woody debris. The area of an ecosystem can vary greatly from tiny to vast. A single tree is of little consequence to the classification of a forest ecosystem, but it is far more significant to smaller organisms. Several generations of an aphid population can exist over the lifespan of a single leaf. Each of those aphids, in turn, support diverse bacterial communities. Tree growth is related to local site variables, such as soil type, moisture content, slope of the land, and forest canopy closure. More complex global factors, such as climate, must be considered for the classification and understanding of processes leading to larger patterns spanning across a forested landscape.

Global patterns of biological diversity are complex. This biocomplexity stems from the interplay among ecological processes that operate and influence patterns that grade into each other, such as transitional areas or ecotones that stretch across different scales. "Complexity in ecology is of at least six distinct types: spatial, temporal, structural, process, behavioural, and geometric." There are different views on what constitutes complexity. One perspective lumps things that we do not understand into this category by virtue of the computational effort it would require to piece together the numerous interacting parts. Alternatively, complexity in life sciences can be viewed as emergent self-organized systems with multiple possible outcomes directed by random accidents of history. Small scale patterns do not necessarily explain large scale phenomena, otherwise captured in the expression 'the sum is greater than the parts'. Ecologists have identified emergent and self-organizing phenomena that operate at different environmental scales of influence, ranging from molecular to planetary, and these require different sets of scientific explanation. Long-term ecological studies provide important track records to better understand the complexity of ecosystems over longer temporal and broader spatial scales. The International Long Term Ecological Network manages and exchanges scientific information among research sites. The longest experiment in existence is the Park Grass Experiment that was initiated in 1856. Another example includes the Hubbard Brook study in operation since 1960.

To structure the study of ecology into a manageable framework of understanding, the biological world is conceptually organized as a nested hierarchy of organization, ranging in scale from genes, to cells, to tissues, to organs, to organisms, to species and up to the level of the biosphere. Together these hierarchical scales of life form a panarchy. Ecosystems are primarily researched at three key levels of organization—organisms, populations, and communities. Ecologists study ecosystems by sampling a certain number of individuals that are representative of a population. Ecosystems consist of communities interacting with each other and the environment. In ecology, communities are created by the interaction of the populations of different species in an area.

Biodiversity is an attribute of a site or area that consists of the variety within and among biotic communities, whether influenced by humans or not, at any spatial scale from microsites and habitat patches to the entire biosphere.

Biodiversity (an abbreviation of biological diversity) describes the diversity of life from genes to ecosystems and spans every level of biological organization. There are many ways to index, measure, and represent biodiversity. Biodiversity includes species diversity, ecosystem diversity, genetic diversity and the complex processes operating at and among these respective levels. Biodiversity plays an important role in ecological health as much as it does for human health. Preventing or prioritizing species extinctions is one way to preserve biodiversity, but populations, the genetic diversity within them and ecological processes, such as migration, are being threatened on global scales and disappearing rapidly as well. Conservation priorities and management techniques require different approaches and considerations to address the full ecological scope of biodiversity. Populations and species migration, for example, are more sensitive indicators of ecosystem services that sustain and contribute natural capital toward the well-being of humanity. An understanding of biodiversity has practical application for ecosystem-based conservation planners as they make ecologically responsible decisions in management recommendations to consultant firms, governments and industry.

There are many definitions of the niche dating back to 1917, but G. Evelyn Hutchinson made conceptual advances in 1957 and introduced the most widely accepted definition: "The niche is the set of biotic and abiotic conditions in which a species is able to persist and maintain stable population sizes." The ecological niche is a central concept in the ecology of organisms and is sub-divided into the *fundamental* and the *realized* niche. The fundamental niche is the set of environmental conditions under which a species is able to persist. The realized niche is the set of environmental plus ecological conditions under which a species persists.

The habitat of a species is a related but distinct concept that describes the environment over which a species is known to occur and the type of community that is formed as a result. More specifically, "habitats can be defined as regions in environmental space that are composed of multiple dimensions, each representing a biotic or abiotic environmental variable; that is, any component or characteristic of the environment related directly (e.g. forage biomass and quality) or indirectly (e.g. elevation) to the use of a location by the animal." For example, the habitat might refer to an aquatic or terrestrial environment that can be further categorized as montane or alpine ecosystems.

Biogeographical patterns and range distributions are explained or predicted through knowledge and understanding of a species traits and niche requirements. Species have functional traits that are uniquely adapted to the ecological niche. A trait is a measurable property of an organism that influences its performance. Traits of each species are suited ar uniquely adapted to their ecological niche. This means that resident species are at an advantage and able to competitively exclude other similarly adapted species from having an overlapping geographic range. This is called the competitive exclusion principle.

Organisms are subject to environmental pressures, but they are also modifiers of their habitats. The regulatory feedback between organisms and their environment can modify conditions from local (e.g., a pond) to global scales (e.g., Gaia), over time and even after death, such as decaying logs or silica skeleton deposits from marine organisms. The process and concept of ecosystem engineering has also been called niche construction. Ecosystem engineers are defined as: "... organisms that directly or indirectly modulate the availability of resources to other species, by causing physical state changes in biotic or abiotic materials. In so doing they modify, maintain and create habitats".

The ecosystem engineering concept has stimulated a new appreciation for the degree of influence that organisms have on the ecosystem and evolutionary process. The terms niche construction are more often used in reference to the under appreciated feedback mechanism of natural selection imparting forces on the abiotic niche. An example of natural selection through ecosystem engineering occurs in the nests of social insects, including ants, bees, wasps, and termites. There is an emergent homeostasis in the structure of the nest that regulates, maintains and defends the physiology of the entire colony. Termite mounds, for example, maintain a constant internal temperature through the design of air-conditioning chimneys. The structure of the nests themselves are subject to the forces of natural selection. Moreover, the nest can survive over successive generations, which means that ancestors inherit both genetic material and a legacy niche that was constructed before their time. Diatoms in the Bay of Fundy, Canada, provide another example of an ecosystem engineer. Benthic diatoms living in estuarine sediments secrete carbohydrate exudates that bind the sand and stabilizes the environment. The diatoms cause a physical state change in the properties of the sand that allows other organisms to colonize the area. The concept of ecosystem engineering brings new conceptual implications for the discipline of conservation biology.

Metapopulation Ecology

Populations are also studied and modelled according to the metapopulation concept. The metapopulation concept was introduced in 1969: "as a population of populations which go extinct locally and recolonize." Metapopulation ecology is another statistical approach that is often used in conservation research. Metapopulation research simplifies the landscape into patches of varying levels of quality.

Metapopulation models have been used to explain life-history evolution, such as the ecological stability of amphibian metamorphosis in small vernal ponds. Alternative ecological strategies have evolved. For example, some salamanders forgo metamorphosis and sexually mature as aquatic neotenes. The seasonal duration of wetlands and the migratory range of the species determines which ponds are connected and if they form a metapopulation. The duration of the life history stages of amphibians relative to the duration of the vernal pool before it dries up regulates the ecological development of metapopulations connecting aquatic patches to terrestrial patches.

In metapopulation terminology there are emigrants (individuals that leave a patch), immigrants (individuals that move into a patch) and sites are classed either as sources or sinks. A site is a generic term that refers to places where ecologists sample populations, such as ponds or defined sampling areas in a forest. Source patches are productive sites that generate a seasonal supply of juveniles that migrate to other patch locations. Sink patches are unproductive sites that only receive migrants and will go extinct unless rescued by an adjacent source patch or environmental conditions become more favourable. Metapopulation models examine patch dynamics over time to answer questions about spatial and demographic ecology. The ecology of metapopulations is a dynamic process of extinction and colonization. Small patches of lower quality (i.e., sinks) are maintained or rescued by a seasonal influx of new immigrants. A dynamic metapopulation structure evolves from year to year, where some patches are sinks in dry years and become sources when conditions are more favorable. Ecologists use a mixture of computer models and field studies to explain metapopulation structure.

Community ecology is a subdiscipline of ecology which studies the distribution, abundance, demography, and interactions between coexisting populations. An example of a study in community ecology might measure primary production in a wetland in relation to decomposition and consumption rates. This requires an understanding of the community connections between plants (i.e., primary producers) and the decomposers (e.g., fungi and bacteria). or the analysis of predator-prey dynamics affecting amphibian biomass. Food webs and trophic levels are two widely employed conceptual models used to explain the linkages among species.

Food Webs

A food web is the archetypal ecological network. They are a type of concept map that illustrate pathways of energy flows in an ecological community, usually starting with solar energy being used by plants during photosynthesis. As plants grow, they accumulate carbohydrates and are eaten by grazing herbivores. Step by step lines or relations are drawn until a web of life is illustrated.

There are different ecological dimensions that can be mapped to create more complicated food webs, including: species composition (type of species), richness (number of species), biomass (the dry weight of plants and animals), productivity (rates of conversion of energy and nutrients into growth), and stability (food webs over time). Microcosm studies are used to simplify food web research into semi-isolated units such as small springs, decaying logs, and laboratory experiments using organisms that reproduce quickly, such as daphnia feeding on algae grown under controlled environments in jars of water.

Principles gleaned from food web microcosm studies are used to extrapolate smaller dynamic concepts to larger systems. Food webs are limited because they are generally restricted to a specific habitat, such as a cave or a pond. The food web only shows a small part of the complexity connecting the aquatic system to the adjacent terrestrial land. Many of these species migrate into other habitats to distribute their effects on a larger scale. In other words, food webs are incomplete, but are nonetheless a valuable tool in understanding community ecosystems.

Food chain length is another way of describing food webs as a measure of the number of species encountered as energy or nutrients move from the plants to top predators. There are different ways of calculating food chain length depending on what parameters of the food web dynamic are being considered: connectance, energy, or interaction. In a simple predator-prey example, a deer is one step removed from the plants it eats (chain length = 1) and a wolf that eats the deer is two steps removed (chain length = 2). The relative amount or strength of influence that these parameters have on the food web address questions about:

- the identity or existence of a few dominant species (called strong interactors or keystone species)
- the total number of species and food-chain length (including many weak interactors); and
- how community structure, function and stability is determined.

Trophic Dynamics

The Greek root of the word *troph*, trophe, means food or feeding. Links in food-webs primarily connect feeding relations or trophism among species. Biodiversity within ecosystems can be organized into vertical and horizontal dimensions. The vertical dimension represents feeding relations that become further removed from the base of the food chain up toward top predators. The horizontal dimension represents the abundance or biomass at each level. When the relative abundance or biomass of each functional feeding group is stacked into their respective trophic levels they naturally sort into a 'pyramid of numbers'. Functional groups are broadly categorized as autotrophs (or primary producers), heterotrophs (or consumers), and detrivores (or decomposers). Heterotrophs can be further sub-divided into different functional groups, including: primary consumers (strict herbivores), secondary consumers (predators that feed exclusively on herbivores) and tertiary consumers (predators that feed on a mix of herbivores and predators). Omnivores do not fit neatly into a functional category because they eat both plant and animal tissues. It has been suggested that omnivores have a greater functional influence as predators because relative to herbivores they are comparatively inefficient at grazing.

Ecologist collect data on trophic levels and food webs to statistically model and mathematically calculate parameters, such as those used in other kinds of network analysis (e.g., graph theory), to study emergent patterns and properties shared among ecosystems. The emergent pyramidal arrangement of trophic levels with amounts of energy transfer decreasing as species become further removed from the source of production is one of several patterns that is repeated amongst the planets ecosystems. The size of each level in the pyramid generally represents biomass, which can be measured as the dry weight of an organism. Autotrophs may have the highest global proportion of biomass, but they are closely rivaled or surpassed by microbes.

The decomposition of dead organic matter, such as leaves falling on the forest floor, turns into soils that feed plant production. The total sum of the planet's soil ecosystems is called the pedosphere where a very large proportion of the Earth's biodiversity sorts into other trophic levels. Invertebrates that feed and shred larger leaves, for example, create smaller bits for smaller organisms in the feeding chain. Collectively, these are the detrivores that regulate soil formation. Tree roots, fungi, bacteria, worms, ants, beetles, centipedes, spiders, mammals, birds, reptiles, amphibians and other less familiar creatures all work to create the trophic web of life in soil ecosystems. As organisms feed and migrate through soils they physically displace materials, which is an important ecological process called bioturbation. Biomass of soil microorganisms are influenced by and feed back into the trophic dynamics of the exposed solar surface ecology. Paleoecological studies of soils places the origin for bioturbation to a time before the Cambrian period. Other events, such as the evolution of trees and amphibians moving into land in the Devonian period played a significant role in the development of soils and ecological trophism.

Functional trophic groups sort out hierarchically into pyramidic trophic levels because it requires specialized adaptations to become a photosynthesizer or a predator, so few organisms have the adaptations needed to combine both abilities. This explains why functional adaptations to trophism (feeding) organizes different species into emergent functional groups. Trophic levels are part of the holistic or complex systems view of ecosystems. Each trophic level contains unrelated species that grouped together because they share common ecological functions. Grouping functionally similar species into a trophic system gives a macroscopic image of the larger functional design.

Links in a food-web illustrate direct trophic relations among species, but there are also indirect effects that can alter the abundance, distribution, or biomass in the trophic levels. For example, predators eating herbivores indirectly influence the control and regulation of primary production in plants. Although the predators do not eat the plants directly, they regulate the population of herbibores that are directly linked to plant trophism. The net effect of direct and indirect relations is called trophic cascades. Trophic cascades are separated into species-level cascades, where only a subset of the food-web dynamic is impacted by a change in population numbers, and community-level cascades, where a change in population numbers has a dramatic effect on the entire food-web, such as the distribution of plant biomass.

Keystone Species

A keystone species is a species that is disproportionately connected to more species in the food-web. Keystone species have lower levels of biomass in the trophic pyramid relative to the importance of their role. The many connections that a keystone species holds means that it maintains the organization and structure of entire communities. The loss of a keystone species results in a range of dramatic cascading effects that alters trophic dynamics, other food-web connections and can cause the extinction of other species in the community.

Sea otters (*Enhydra lutris*) are commonly cited as an example of a keystone species because they limit the density of sea urchins that feed on kelp. If sea otters are removed from the system, the urchins graze until the kelp beds disappear and this has a dramatic effect on community structure. Hunting of sea otters, for example, is thought to have indirectly led to the extinction of the Steller's Sea Cow (*Hydrodamalis gigas*). While the keystone species concept has been used extensively as a conservation tool, it has been criticized for being poorly defined from an operational stance. It is very difficult to experimentally determine in each different ecosystem what species may hold a keystone role. Furthermore, food-web theory suggests that keystone species may not be all that common. It is therefore unclear how generally the keystone species model can be applied.

Ecosystem Ecology

These ecosystems, as we may call them, are of the most various kinds and sizes. They form one category of the multitudinous physical systems of the universe, which range from the universe as a whole down to the atom.

Tansley

The concept of the ecosystem was first introduced in 1935 to describe habitats within biomes that form an integrated whole and a dynamically responsive system having both physical and biological complexes. Within an ecosystem there are inseparable ties that link organisms to the physical and biological components of their environment to which they are adapted. Ecosystems are complex adaptive systems where the interaction of life processes form self-organizing patterns across different scales of time and space. This section introduces key areas of ecosystem ecology that are used to inquire, understand and explain observed patterns of biodiversity and ecosystem function across different scales of organization.

The Biome

Ecological units of organization are defined through reference to any magnitude of space and time on the planet. Communities of organisms, for example, are somewhat arbitrarily defined, but the processes of life integrate at different levels and organize into more complex wholes. Biomes, for example, are a larger unit of organization that categorize regions of the Earth's ecosystems mainly according to the structure and composition of vegetation. Different researchers have applied different methods to define continental boundaries of biomes dominated by different functional types of vegetative communities that are limited in distribution by climate, precipitation, weather and other environmental variables. Examples of biome names include: tropical rainforest, temperate broadleaf and mixed forests, temperate deciduous forest, taiga, tundra, hot desert, and polar desert. Other researchers have recently started to categorize other types of biomes, such as the human and oceanic microbiomes. To a microbe, the human body is a habitat and a landscape. The microbiome has been largely discovered through advances in molecular genetics that have revealed a hidden richness of microbial diversity on the planet. The oceanic microbiome plays a significant role in the ecological biogeochemistry of the planet's oceans.

The Biosphere

Ecological theory has been used to explain self-emergent regulatory phenomena at the planetary scale. The largest scale of ecological organization is the biosphere: the total sum of ecosystems on the planet. Ecological relations regulate the flux of energy, nutrients, and climate all the way up to the planetary scale. For example, the dynamic history of the planetary CO_2 and O_2 composition of the atmosphere has been largely determined by the biogenic flux of gases coming from respiration and photosynthesis, with levels fluctuating over time and in relation to the ecology and evolution of plants and animals. When sub-component parts are organized into a whole there are oftentimes emergent properties that describe the nature of the system. This the Gaia hypothesis, and is an example of holism applied in ecological theory. The ecology of the planet acts as a single regulatory or holistic unit called Gaia. The Gaia hypothesis states that there is an emergent feedback loop generated by the metabolism of living organisms that maintains the temperature of the Earth and atmospheric conditions within a narrow self-regulating range of tolerance.

Relation to Evolution

Ecology and evolution are considered sister disciplines of the life sciences. Natural selection, life history, development, adaptation, populations, and inheritance are examples of concepts that thread equally into ecological and evolutionary theory. Morphological, behavioural and/or genetic traits, for example, can be mapped onto evolutionary trees to study the historical development of a species in relation to their functions and roles in different ecological circumstances. In this framework, the analytical tools of ecologists and evolutionists overlap as they organize, classify and investigate life through common systematic principals, such as phylogenetics or the Linnaean system of taxonomy. The two disciplines often appear together, such as in the title of the journal *Trends in Ecology and Evolution*. There is no sharp boundary separating ecology from evolution and they differ more in their areas of applied focus. Both disciplines discover and explain emergent and unique properties and processes operating across different spatial or temporal scales of organization. While the boundary between ecology and evolution is not always clear, it is understood that ecologists study the abiotic and biotic factors that influence the evolutionary process.

All organisms are motile to some extent. Even plants express complex behaviour, including memory and communication. Behavioural ecology is the study of ethology and its ecological and evolutionary implications. Ethology is the study of observable movement or behaviour in nature. This could include investigations of motile sperm of plants, mobile phytoplankton, zooplankton swimming toward the female egg, the cultivation of fungi by weevils, the mating dance of a salamander, or social gatherings of amoeba.

Adaptation is the central unifying concept in behavioural ecology."International Society for Behavioural Ecology". Behaviours can be recorded as traits and inherited in much the same way that eye and hair color can. Behaviours evolve and become adapted to the ecosystem because they are subject to the forces of natural selection. Hence, behaviours can be adaptive, meaning that they evolve functional utilities that increases reproductive success for the individuals that inherit such traits. This is also the technical definition for fitness in biology, which is a measure of reproductive success over successive generations.

Predator-prey interactions are an introductory concept into food-web studies as well as behavioural ecology. Prey species can exhibit different kinds of behavioural adaptations to predators, such as avoid, flee or defend. Many prey species are faced with multiple predators that differ in the degree of danger posed. To be adapted to their environment and face predatory threats, organisms must balance their energy budgets as they invest in different aspects of their life history, such as growth, feeding, mating, socializing, or modifying their habitat. Hypotheses posited in behavioural ecology are generally based on adaptive principals of conservation, optimization or efficiency. For example:

- "The threat-sensitive predator avoidance hypothesis predicts that prey should assess the degree of threat posed by different predators and match their behaviour according to current levels of risk".
- "The optimal flight initiation distance occurs where expected postencounter fitness is maximized, which depends on the prey's initial fitness, benefits obtainable by not fleeing, energetic escape costs, and expected fitness loss due to predation risk".

The behaviour of long-toed salamanders (*Ambystoma macrodactylum*) presents an example in this context. When threatened, the long-toed salamander defends itself by waving its tail and secreting a white milky fluid. The excreted fluid is distasteful, toxic and adhesive, but it is also used for nutrient and energy storage during hibernation. Hence, salamanders subjected to frequent predatory attack will be energetically compromised as they use up their energy stores.

Ecological interactions can be divided into host and associate relationships. A host is any entity that harbors another that is called the associate Host and associate relationships among species that are mutually or reciprocally beneficial are called mutualisms. If the host and associate are physically connected, the relationship is called symbiosis. Approximately 60 per cent of all plants, for example, have a symbiotic relationship with arbuscular mycorrhizal fungi. Symbiotic plants and fungi exchange carbohydrates for mineral nutrients.

Symbiosis differs from indirect mutualisms where the organisms live apart. For example, tropical rainforests regulate the Earth's atmosphere. Trees living in the equatorial regions of the planet supply oxygen into the atmosphere that sustains species living in distant polar regions of the planet. This relationship is called commensalism because many other host species receive the benefits of clean air at no cost or harm to the associate tree species supplying the oxygen. The host and associate relationship is called parasitism if one species benefits while the other suffers. Competition among species or among members of the same species is defined as reciprocal antagonism, such as grasses competing for growth space.

Popular ecological study systems for mutualism include, fungus-growing ants employing agricultural symbiosis, bacteria living in the guts of insects and other organisms, the fig wasp and yucca moth pollination complex, lichens with fungi and photosynthetic algae, and corals with photosynthetic algae.

Intraspecific behaviours are notable in the social insects, slime moulds, social spiders, human society, and naked mole rats where eusocialism has evolved. Social behaviours include reciprocally beneficial behaviours among kin and nest mates. Social behaviours evolve from kin and group selection. Kin selection explains altruism through genetic relationships, whereby an altruistic behaviour leading to death is rewarded by the survival of genetic copies distributed among surviving relatives. The social insects, including ants, bees and wasps are most famously studied for this type of relationship because the male drones are clones that share the same genetic make-up as every other male in the colony In contrast, group selectionists find examples of altruism among non-genetic relatives and explain this through selection acting on the group, whereby it becomes selectively advantageous for groups if their members express altruistic behaviours to one another. Groups that are predominantely altruists beat groups that are predominantely selfish.

A often quoted behavioural ecology hypothesis is known as Lack's brood reduction hypothesis (named after David Lack). Lack's hypothesis posits an evolutionary and ecological explanation as to why birds lay a series of eggs with an asynchronous delay leading to nestlings of mixed age and weights. According to Lack, this brood behaviour is an ecological insurance that allows the larger birds to survive in poor years and all birds to survive when food is plentiful.

Elaborate sexual displays and posturing are encountered in the behavioural ecology of animals. The birds of paradise, for example, display elaborate ornaments and song during courtship. These displays serve a dual purpose of signalling healthy or well-adapted individuals and good genes. The elaborate displays are driven by sexual selection as an advertisement of quality of traits among male suitors.

Biogeography

The word *biogeography* is an amalgamation of *biology* and *geography*. Biogeography is the comparative study of the geographic distribution of organisms and the corresponding evolution of their traits in space and time. The Journal of Biogeography was established in 1974. Biogeography and ecology share many of their disciplinary roots. For example, the theory of island biogeography, published by the mathematician Robert MacArthur and ecologist Edward O. Wilson in 1967 is considered one of the fundamentals of ecological theory.

Biogeography has a long history in the natural sciences where questions arise concerning the spatial distribution of plants and animals. Ecology and evolution provide the explanatory context for biogeographical studies. Biogeographical patterns result from ecological processes that influence range distributions, such as migration and dispersal. and from historical processes that split populations or species into different areas. The biogeographic processes that result in the natural splitting of species explains much of the modern distribution of the Earth's biota. The splitting of lineages in a species is called vicariance biogeography and it is a sub-discipline of biogeography. There are also practical applications in the field of biogeography concerning ecological systems and processes. For example, the range and distribution of biodiversity and invasive species responding to climate change is a serious concern and active area of research in context of global warming.

r/K-Selection Theory

A population ecology concept (introduced in MacArthur and Wilson's (1967) book, *The Theory of Island Biogeography*) is *r/K* selection theory, one of the first predictive models in ecology used to explain life-history evolution.

The premise behind the *r/K* selection model is that natural selection pressures change according to population density. For example, when an island is first colonized, density of individuals is low. The initial increase in population size is *not* limited by competition, leaving an abundance of available resources for rapid population growth. These early phases of population growth experience *density-independent* forces of natural selection, which is called *r*-selection. As the population becomes more crowded, it approaches the island's carrying capacity, thus forcing individuals to compete more heavily for fewer available resources. Under crowded conditions the population experiences density-dependent forces of natural selection, called *K*-selection.

In the *r/K*-selection model, the first variable *r* is the intrinsic rate of natural increase in population size and the second variable *K* is the carrying capacity of a population. Different species evolve different life-history strategies spanning a continuum between these two selective forces. An *r*-selected species is one that has high birth rates, low levels of parental investment, and high rates of mortality before individuals reach maturity. Evolution favours high rates of fecundity in *r*-selected species. Many kinds of insects and invasive species exhibit *r*-selected characteristics. In contrast, a *K*-selected species has low rates of fecundity, high levels of parental investment in the young, and low rates of mortality as individuals mature. Humans and elephants are examples of species exhibiting *K*-selected characteristics, including longevity and efficiency in the conversion of more resources into fewer offspring.

Molecular Ecology

The important relationship between ecology and genetic inheritance predates modern techniques for molecular analysis. Molecular ecological research became more feasible with the development of rapid and accessible genetic technologies, such as the polymerase chain reaction (PCR). The rise of molecular technologies and influx of research questions into this new ecological field resulted in the publication *Molecular Ecology* in 1992. Molecular ecology uses various analytical techniques to study genes in an evolutionary and ecological context. In 1994, professor John Avise also played a leading role in this area of science with the publication of his book, *Molecular Markers, Natural History and Evolution*. Newer technologies opened a wave of genetic analysis into organisms once difficult to study from an ecological or evolutionary standpoint, such as bacteria, fungi and nematodes.

Molecular ecology engendered a new research paradigm to investigate ecological questions considered otherwise intractable. Molecular investigations revealed previously obscured details in the tiny intricacies of nature and improved resolution into probing questions about behavioural and biogeographical ecology. For example, molecular ecology revealed promiscuous sexual behaviour and multiple male partners in tree swallows previously thought to be socially monogamous. In a biogeographical context, the marriage between genetics, ecology and evolution resulted in a new sub-discipline called phylogeography.

Relation to the Environment

The environment is dynamically interlinked, imposed upon and constrains organisms at any time throughout their life cycle. Like the term ecology, environment has different conceptual meanings and to many these terms also overlap with the concept of *nature*. Environment "...includes the physical world, the social world of human relations and the built world of human creation." The environment in ecosystems includes both physical parameters and biotic attributes. The physical environment is external to the level of biological organization under investigation, including abiotic factors such as temperature, radiation, light, chemistry, climate and geology. The biotic environment includes genes, cells, organisms, members of the same species (conspecifics) and other species that share a habitat. The laws of thermodynamics applies to ecology by means of its physical state. Armed with an understanding of metabolic and thermodynamic principles a complete accounting of energy and material flow can be traced through an ecosystem.

Environmental and ecological relations are studied through reference to conceptually manageable and isolated parts. Once the effective environmental components are understood they conceptually link back together as a *holocoenotic* system. In other words, the organism and the environment form a dynamic whole (or umwelt). Change in one ecological or environmental factor can concurrently affect the dynamic state of an entire ecosystem.

Ecological studies are necessarily holistic as opposed to reductionistic. Holism has three scientific meanings or uses that identify with:

1. the mechanistic complexity of ecosystems;
2. the practical description of patterns in quantitative reductionist terms where correlations may be identified but nothing is understood about the causal relations without reference to the whole system;
3. a metaphysical hierarchy whereby the causal relations of larger systems are understood without reference to the smaller parts.

An example of the metaphysical aspect to holism is the trend of increased exterior thickness in shells of different species. The reason for a thickness increase can be understood through reference to principals of natural selection via predation without any reference to the biomolecular properties of the exterior shells.

Metabolism and the Early Atmosphere

Metabolism — the rate at which energy and material resources are taken up from the environment, transformed within an organism, and allocated to maintenance, growth and reproduction — is a fundamental physiological trait.

The Earth formed approximately 4.5 billion years ago and environmental conditions were too extreme for life to form for the first 500 million years. During this early Hadean period, the Earth started to cool, allowing a crust and oceans to form. Environmental conditions were unsuitable for the origins of life for the first billion years after the Earth formed. The Earth's atmosphere transformed from being dominated by hydrogen, to one composed mostly of methane and ammonia. Over the next billion years the metabolic activity of life transformed the atmosphere to higher concentrations of carbon dioxide, nitrogen, and water vapour. These gases changed the way that light from the sun hit the Earth's surface and greenhouse effects trapped heat. There were untapped sources of free energy within the mixture of reducing and oxidizing gasses that set the stage for primitive ecosystems to evolve and, in turn, the atmosphere also evolved.

The biology of life operates within a certain range of temperatures. Heat is a form of energy that regulates temperature. Heat affects growth rates, activity, behaviour and primary production. Temperature is largely dependent on the incidence of solar radiation. The latitudinal and longitudinal spatial variation of temperature greatly affects climates and consequently the distribution of biodiversity and levels of primary production in different ecosystems or biomes across the planet. Heat and temperature relate importantly to metabolic activity. Poikilotherms, for example, have a body temperature that is largely regulated and dependent on the temperature of the external environment. In contrast, homeotherms regulate their internal body temperature by expending metabolic energy.

There is a relationship between light, primary production, and ecological energy budgets. Sunlight is the primary input of energy into the planet's ecosystems. Light is composed of electromagnetic energy of different wavelengths. Radiant energy from the sun generates heat, provides photons of light measured as active energy in the chemical reactions of life, and also acts as a catalyst for genetic mutation. Plants, algae, and some bacteria absorb light and assimilate the energy through photosynthesis. Organisms capable of assimilating energy by photosynthesis or through inorganic fixation of H_2S are autotrophs. Autotrophs—responsible for primary production–assimilate light energy that becomes metabolically stored as potential energy in the form of biochemical enthalpic bonds.

The rate of diffusion of carbon dioxide and oxygen is approximately 10,000 times slower in water than it is in air. When soils become flooded, they quickly lose oxygen from low-concentration (hypoxic) to an (anoxic) environment where anaerobic bacteria thrive among the roots. Water also influences the spectral properties of light that becomes more diffuse as it is reflected off the water surface and submerged particles. Aquatic plants exhibit a wide variety of morphological and physiological adaptations that allow them to survive, compete and diversify these environments. For example, the roots and stems develop large cellular air spaces to allow for the efficient transportation gases (for example, CO_2 and O_2) used in respiration and photosynthesis. In drained soil, microorganisms use oxygen during respiration. In aquatic environments, anaerobic soil microorganisms use nitrate, manganic ions, ferric ions, sulfate, carbon dioxide and some organic compounds. The activity of soil microorganisms and the chemistry of the water reduces the oxidation-reduction potentials of the water. Carbon dioxide, for example, is reduced to methane (CH_4) by methanogenic bacteria. Salt water also requires special physiological adaptations to deal with water loss. Salt water plants (or halophytes) are able to osmo-regulate their internal salt (NaCl) concentrations or develop special organs for shedding salt away. The physiology of fish is also specially adapted to deal with high levels of salt through osmoregulation. Their gills form electrochemical gradients that mediate salt excrusion in salt water and uptake in fresh water.

Gravity

The shape and energy of the land is affected to a large degree by gravitational forces. On a larger scale, the distribution of gravitational forces on the earth are uneven and influence the shape and movement of tectonic plates as well as having an influence on geomorphic processes such as orogeny and erosion. These forces govern many of the geophysical properties and distributions of ecological biomes across the Earth. On an organism scale, gravitational forces provide directional cues for plant and fungal growth (gravitropism), orientation cues for animal migrations, and influence the biomechanics and size of animals. Ecological traits, such as allocation of biomass in trees during growth are subject to mechanical failure as gravitational forces influence the position and structure of branches and leaves. The cardiovascular systems of all animals are functionally adapted to overcome pressure and gravitational forces that change according to the features of organisms (e.g., height, size, shape), their behaviour (e.g., diving, running, flying), and the habitat occupied (e.g., water, hot deserts, cold tundra).

Pressure

Climatic and osmotic pressure places physiological constraints on organisms, such as flight and respiration at high altitudes, or diving to deep ocean depths. These constraints influence vertical limits of ecosystems in the biosphere as organisms are physiologically sensitive and adapted to atmospheric and osmotic water pressure differences. Oxygen levels, for example, decrease with increasing pressure and are a limiting factor for life at higher altitudes. Water transportation through trees is another important ecophysiological parameter dependent upon pressure. Water pressure in the depths of oceans requires adaptations to deal with the different living conditions. Mammals, such as whales, dolphins and seals are adapted to deal with changes in sound due to water pressure differences.

Wind and Turbulence

The architecture of inflorescence in grasses is subject to the physical pressures of wind and shaped by the forces of natural selection facilitating wind-pollination (or anemophily).

Turbulent forces in air and water have significant effects on the environment and ecosystem distribution, form and dynamics. On a planetary scale, ecosystems are affected by circulation patterns in the global trade winds. Wind power and the turbulent forces it creates can influence heat, nutrient, and biochemical profiles of ecosystems. For example, wind running over the surface of a lake creates turbulence, mixing the water column and influencing the environmental profile to create thermally layered zones, partially governing how fish, algae, and other parts of the aquatic ecology are structured. Wind speed and turbulence also exert influence on rates of evapotranspiration rates and energy budgets in plants and animals. Wind speed, temperature and moisture content can vary as winds travel across different landfeatures and elevations. The westerlies, for example, come into contact with the coastal and interior mountains of western North America to produce a rain shadow on the leeward side of the mountain. The air expands and moisture condenses as the winds move up in elevation which can cause precipitation; this is called orographic lift. This environmental process produces spatial divisions in biodiversity, as species adapted to wetter conditions are range-restricted to the coastal mountain valleys and unable to migrate across the xeric ecosystems of the Columbia Basin to intermix with sister lineages that are segregated to the interior mountain systems.

Plants convert carbon dioxide into biomass and emit oxygen into the atmosphere. Approximately 350 million years ago (near the Devonian period) the photosynthetic process brought the concentration of atmospheric oxygen above 17 per cent, which allowed combustion to occur. Fire releases CO_2 and converts fuel into ash and tar. Fire is a significant ecological parameter that raises many issues pertaining to its control and suppression in management. While the issue of fire in relation to ecology and plants has been recognized for a long time, Charles Cooper brought attention to the issue of forest fires in relation to the ecology of forest fire suppression and management in the 1960s.

Fire creates environmental mosaics and a patchiness to ecosystem age and canopy structure. Native North Americans were among the first to influence fire regimes by controlling their spread near their homes or by lighting fires to stimulate the production of herbaceous foods and basketry materials. The altered state of soil nutrient supply and cleared canopy structure also opens new ecological niches for seedling establishment. Most ecosystem are adapted to natural fire cycles. Plants, for example, are equipped with a variety of adaptations to deal with forest fires. Some species (e.g., *Pinus halepensis*) cannot germinate until after their seeds have lived through a fire. This environmental trigger for seedlings is called serotiny. Some compounds from smoke also promote seed germination.

Biogeochemistry

Ecologists study and measure nutrient budgets to understand how these materials are regulated and flow through the environment. This research has led to an understanding that there is a global feedback between ecosystems and the physical parameters of this planet including minerals, soil, pH, ions, water and atmospheric gases. There are six major elements, including H (hydrogen), C (carbon), N (nitrogen), O (oxygen), S (sulfur), and P (phosphorus) that form the constitution of all biological macromolecules and feed into the Earth's geochemical processes. From the smallest scale of biology the combined effect of billions upon billions of ecological processes amplify and ultimately regulate the biogeochemical cycles of the Earth. Understanding the relations and cycles mediated between these elements and their ecological pathways has significant bearing toward understanding global biogeochemistry.

The ecology of global carbon budgets gives one example of the linkage between biodiversity and biogeochemistry. For starters, the Earth's oceans are estimated to hold 40,000 gigatonnes (Gt) carbon, vegetation and soil is estimated to hold 2070 Gt carbon, and fossil fuel emissions are estimated to emit an annual flux of 6.3 Gt carbon. At different times in the Earth's history there has been major restructuring in these global carbon budgets that was regulated to a large extent by the ecology of the land. For example, through the early-mid Eocene volcanic outgassing, the oxidation of methane stored in wetlands, and seafloor gases increased atmospheric CO_2 concentrations to levels as high as 3500 ppm. In the Oligocene, from 25 to 32 million years ago, there was another significant restructuring in the global carbon cycle as grasses evolved a special type of C4 photosynthesis and expanded their ranges. This new photosynthetic pathway evolved in response to the drop in atmospheric CO_2 concentrations below 550 ppm. Ecosystem functions such as these feedback significantly into global atmospheric models for carbon cycling. Loss in the abundance and distribution of biodiversity causes global carbon cycle feedbacks that are expected to increase rates of global warming in the next century. The effect of global warming melting large sections of permafrost creates a new mosaic of flooded areas where decomposition results in the emission of methane (CH_4). Hence, there is a relationship between global warming, decomposition and respiration in soils and wetlands producing significant climate feedbacks and altered global biogeochemical cycles. There is concern over increases in atmospheric methane in the context of the global carbon cycle, because methane is also a greenhouse gas that is 23 times more effective at absorbing long-wave radiation on a 100 year time scale.

Unlike many scientific disciplines, ecology has a complex origin due in large part to its interdisciplinary nature. Several published books provide extensive coverage of the classics. In the early 20th century, ecology was an analytical form of natural history The descriptive nature of natural history included examination of the interaction of organisms with both their environment and their community. Such examinations, conducted by important natural historians including James Hutton and Jean-Baptiste Lamarck, contributed to the development of ecology. The term 'ecology' is a more recent scientific development and was first coined by the German biologist Ernst Haeckel in his book *Generelle Morphologie der Organismen* (1866).

By ecology we mean the body of knowledge concerning the economy of nature-the investigation of the total relations of the animal both to its inorganic and its organic environment; including, above all, its friendly and inimical relations with those animals and plants with which it comes directly or indirectly into contact-in a word, ecology is the study of all those complex interrelations referred to by Darwin as the conditions of the struggle of existence.

Opinions differ on who was the founder of modern ecological theory. Some mark Haeckel's definition as the beginning, others say it was Eugenius Warming with the writing of Oecology of Plants: An Introduction to the Study of Plant Communities (1895). Ecology may also be thought to have begun with Carl Linnaeus' research principals on the economy of nature that matured in the early 18th century. He founded an early branch of ecological study he called the economy of nature. The works of Linnaeus influenced Darwin in *The Origin of Species* where he adopted the usage of Linnaeus' phrase on the *economy or polity of nature*. Linnaeus made the first to attempt to define *the balance of nature*, which had previously been held as an assumption rather than formulated as a testable hypothesis. Haeckel, who admired Darwin's work, defined ecology in reference to the economy of nature which has led some to question if ecology is synonymous with Linnaeus' concepts for the economy of nature. Biogeographer Alexander von Humbolt was also foundational and was among the first to recognize ecological gradients and alluded to the modern ecological law of species to area relationships.

The modern synthesis of ecology is a young science, which first attracted substantial formal attention at the end of the 19th century (around the same time as evolutionary studies) and become even more popular during the 1960s environmental movement, though many observations, interpretations and discoveries relating to ecology extend back to much earlier studies in natural history. For example, the concept on the balance or regulation of nature can be traced back to Herodotos (died *c*. 425 BC) who described an early account of mutualism along the Nile river where crocodiles open their mouths to beneficially allow sandpipers safe access to remove leeches. In the broader contributions to the historical development of the ecological sciences, Aristotle is considered one of the earliest naturalists who had an influential role in the philosophical development of ecological sciences. One of Aristotle's students, Theophrastus, made astute ecological observations about plants and posited a philosophical stance about the autonomous relations between plants and their environment that is more in line with modern ecological thought. Both Aristotle and Theophrastus made extensive observations on plant and animal migrations, biogeography, physiology, and their habits in what might be considered an analog of the modern ecological niche. The layout of the first ecological experiment, noted by Charles Darwin in *'The Origin of Species'*, was studied in a grass garden at Woburn Abbey in 1817. The experiment studied the performance of different mixtures of species planted in different kinds of soils.

From Aristotle to Darwin the natural world was predominantly considered static and unchanged since its original creation. Prior to *The Origin of Species* there was little appreciation or understanding of the dynamic and reciprocal relations between organisms, their adaptations and their modifications to the environment. While Charles Darwin is most notable for his treatise on evolution, he is also one of the founders of soil ecology. In *'The Origin of Species'* Darwin also made note of the first ecological experiment that was published in 1816. In the science leading up to Darwin the notion of evolving species was gaining popular support. This scientific paradigm changed the way that researchers approached the ecological sciences.

Nowhere can one see more clearly illustrated what may be called the sensibility of such an organic complex,—expressed by the fact that whatever affects any species belonging to it, must speedily have its influence of some sort upon the whole assemblage. He will thus be made to see the impossibility of studying any form completely, out of relation to the other forms,—the necessity for taking a comprehensive survey of the whole as a condition to a satisfactory understanding of any part.

After the Turn of 20th Century

The first American ecology book was published in 1905 by Frederic Clements. In his book, Clements forwarded the idea of plant communities as a superorganism. This publication launched a debate between ecological holism and individualism that lasted until the 1970s. The Clements superorganism concept proposed that ecosystems progress through regular and determined stages of seral development that are analogous to developmental stages of an organism whose parts function to maintain the integrity of the whole. The Clementsian paradigm was challenged by Henry Gleason. According to Gleason, ecological communities develop from the unique and coincidental association of individual organisms. This perceptual shift placed the focus back onto the life histories of individual organisms and how this relates to the development of community associations.

The Clementsian superorganism concept has not been completely rejected, but it was an overextended application of holism, which remains a significant theme in contemporary ecological studies. Holism was first introduced in 1926 by a polarizing historical figure, a South African General named Jan Christian Smuts. Smuts was inspired by Clement's superorganism theory when he developed and published on the unifying concept of holism, which runs in stark contrast to his racial views as the father of apartheid. Around the same time, Charles Elton pioneered the concept of food chains in his classical book 'Animal Ecology'. Elton defined ecological relations using concepts of food-chains, food-cycles, food-size, and described numerical relations among different functional groups and their relative abundance. Elton's term 'food-cycle' was replaced by 'food-web' in a subsequent ecological text. Elton's book broke conceptual ground by illustrating complex ecological relations through simpler food-web diagrams.

The number of authors publishing on the topic of ecology has grown considerably since the turn of 20th century. The explosion of information available to the modern researcher of ecology makes it an impossible task for one individual to sift through the entire history. Hence, the identification of classics in the history of ecology is a difficult designation to make.

Parallel Development

Ecology has developers in many nations, including Russia's Vladimir Vernadsky and his founding of the biosphere concept in the 1920s or Japan's Kinji Imanishi and his concepts of harmony in nature and habitat segregation in the 1950s. The scientific recognition or importance of contributions to ecology from other cultures is hampered by language and translation barriers. The history of ecology remains an active area of study, often published in the Journal of the History of Biology.

The ecosystems of planet Earth are coupled to human environments. Ecosystems regulate the global geophysical cycles of energy, climate, soil nutrients, and water that in turn support and grow natural capital (including the environmental, physiological, cognitive, cultural, and spiritual dimensions of life). Ultimately, every manufactured product in human environments comes from natural systems. Ecosystems are considered common-pool resources because ecosystems do not exclude beneficiaries and they can be depleted or degraded. For example, green space within communities provides common-pool health services. Research shows that people who are more engaged with regular access to natural areas have lower rates of diabetes, heart disease and psychological disorders. These ecological health services are regularly depleted through urban development projects that do not factor in the common-pool value of ecosystems.

The ecological commons delivers a diverse supply of community services that sustains the well-being of human society. The Millennium Ecosystem Assessment, an international UN initiative involving more than 1,360 experts worldwide, identifies four main ecosystem service types having 30 subcategories stemming from natural capital. The ecological commons includes provisioning (e.g., food, raw materials, medicine, water supplies), regulating (e.g., climate, water, soil retention, flood retention), cultural (e.g., science and education, artistic, spiritual), and supporting (e.g., soil formation, nutrient cycling, water cycling) services.

Policy and human institutions should rarely assume that human enterprise is benign. A safer assumption holds that human enterprise almost always exacts an ecological toll — a debit taken from the ecological commons.

Ecological economics is an economic science that uses many of the same terms and methods that are used in accounting. Natural capital is the stock of materials or information stored in biodiversity that generates services that can enhance the welfare of communities. Population losses are the more sensitive indicator of natural capital than are species extinction in the accounting of ecosystem services. The prospect for recovery in the economic crisis of nature is grim. Populations, such as local ponds and patches of forest are being cleared away and lost at rates that exceed species extinctions.

While we are used to thinking of cities as geographically discrete places, most of the land 'occupied' by their residents lies far beyond their borders. The total area of land required to sustain an urban region (its 'ecological footprint') is typically at least an order of magnitude greater than that contained within municipal boundaries or the associated built-up area.

The WWF 2008 living planet report and other researchers report that human civilization has exceeded the bio-regenerative capacity of the planet. This means that human consumption is extracting more natural resources than can be replenished by ecosystems around the world. In 1992, professor William Rees developed the concept of our ecological footprint. The ecological footprint is a way of accounting the level of impact that human development is having on the Earth's ecosystems. All indications are that the human enterprise is unsustainable as the ecological footprint of society is placing too much stress on the ecology of the planet. The mainstream growth-based economic system adopted by governments worldwide does not include a price or markets for natural capital. This type of economic system places further ecological debt onto future generations.

Human societies are increasingly being placed under stress as the ecological commons is diminished through an accounting system that has incorrectly assumed ". . . that nature is a fixed, indestructible capital asset." While nature is resilient and it does regenerate, there are limits to what can be extracted, but conventional monetary analyses are unable to detect the problem. Evidence of the limits in natural capital are found in the global assessments of biodiversity, which indicate that the current epoch, the

Anthropocene is a sixth mass extinction. Species loss is accelerating at 100-1000 times faster than average background rates in the fossil record. The ecology of the planet has been radically transformed by human society and development causing massive loss of ecosystem services that otherwise deliver and freely sustain equitable benefits to human society through the ecological commons. The ecology of the planet is further threatened by global warming, but investments in nature conservation can provide a regulatory feedback to store and regulate carbon and other greenhouse gases. The field of conservation biology involves ecologists that are researching the nature of the biodiversity threat and searching for solutions to sustain the planet's ecosystems for future generations.

Many human-nature interactions occur indirectly due to the production and use of human-made (manufactured and synthesized) products, such as electronic appliances, furniture, plastics, airplanes, and automobiles. These products insulate humans from the natural environment, leading them to perceive less dependence on natural systems than is the case, but all manufactured products ultimately come from natural systems.

"Human activities are associated directly or indirectly with nearly every aspect of the current extinction spasm".

The current wave of threats, including massive extinction rates and concurrent loss of natural capital to the detriment of human society, is happening rapidly. This is called a biodiversity crisis, because 50 per cent of the worlds species are predicted to go extinct within the next 50 years. The world's fisheries are facing dire challenges as the threat of global collapse appears imminent, with serious ramifications for the well-being of humanity. Governments of the G8 met in 2007 and set forth The Economics of Ecosystems and Biodiversity (TEEB) initiative.

In a global study we will initiate the process of analyzing the global economic benefit of biological diversity, the costs of the loss of biodiversity and the failure to take protective measures versus the costs of effective conservation.

Ecologists are teaming up with economists to measure the wealth of ecosystems and to express their value as a way of finding solutions to the biodiversity crisis. Some researchers have attempted to place a dollar figure on ecosystem services, such as the value that the Canadian boreal forest is contributing to global ecosystem services. If ecologically intact, the boreal forest has an estimated value of US$3.7 trillion. The boreal forest ecosystem is one of the planet's great atmospheric regulators and it stores more carbon than any other biome on the planet. The annual value for ecological services of the Boreal Forest is estimated at US$93.2 billion, or 2.5 greater than the annual value of resource extraction. The economic value of 17 ecosystem services for the entire biosphere (calculated in 1997) has an estimated average value of US$33 trillion ($10^{12}$) per year. These ecological economic values are not currently included in calculations of national income accounts, the GDP and they have no price attributes because they exist mostly outside of the global markets. The loss of natural capital continues to accelerate and goes undetected by mainstream monetary analysis.

CHAPTER 2
Population

A population is all the organisms that both belong to the same species and live in the same geographical area. The area that is used to define the population is such that inter-breeding is possible between any pair within the area and more probable than cross-breeding with individuals from other areas. Normally breeding is substantially more common within the area than across the border.

In sociology, a collection of human beings. Statistical study of human populations occurs within the discipline of demography. This article refers mainly to human population.

According to papers published by the United States Census Bureau, the world population hit 6.5 billion (6,500,000,000) on 24 February 2006. The United Nations Population Fund designated 12 October 1999 as the approximate day on which world population reached 6 billion. This was about 12 years after world population reached 5 billion in 1987, and 6 years after world population reached 5.5 billion in 1993. The population of some countries, such as Nigeria and China is not even known to the nearest million, so there is a considerable margin of error in such estimates.

Population growth increased significantly as the Industrial Revolution gathered pace from 1700 onwards. The last 50 years have seen a yet more rapid increase in the rate of population growth due to medical advances and substantial increases in agricultural productivity, particularly beginning in the 1960s, made by the Green Revolution. In 2007 the United Nations Population Division projected that the world's population will likely surpass 10 billion in 2055. In the future, world population has been expected to reach a peak of growth, from there it will decline due to economic reasons, health concerns, land exhaustion and environmental hazards. There is around an

85 per cent chance that the world's population will stop growing before the end of the century. There is a 60 per cent probability that the world's population will not exceed 10 billion people before 2100, and around a 15 per cent probability that the world's population at the end of the century will be lower than it is today. For different regions, the date and size of the peak population will vary considerably.

The population pattern of less-developed regions of the world in recent years has been marked by gradually declining birth rates following an earlier sharp reduction in death rates. This transition from high birth and death rates to low birth and death rates is often referred to as the demographic transition.

Human population control is the practice of curtailing population increase, usually by reducing the birth rate. Surviving records from Ancient Greece document the first known examples of population control. These include the colonization movement, which saw Greek outposts being built across the Mediterranean and Black Sea basins to accommodate the excess population of individual states. Infanticide and abortion were encouraged in some Greek city states in order to keep population down.

An important example of mandated population control is People's Republic of China's one-child policy, in which having more than one child is made extremely unattractive. This has led to allegations that practices like forced abortions, forced sterilization, and infanticide are used as a result of the policy. The country's sex ratio at birth of 114 boys to 100 girls may be evidence that the latter is often sex-selective.

It is helpful to distinguish between fertility control as individual decision-making and population control as a governmental or state-level policy of regulating population growth. Fertility control may occur when individuals or couples or families take steps to decrease or to regulate the timing of their own child-bearing. In Ansley Coale's oft-cited formulation, three preconditions for a sustained decline in fertility are:

1. acceptance of calculated choice (as opposed to fate or chance or divine will) as a valid element in fertility;
2. perceived advantages from reduced fertility; and
3. knowledge and mastery of effective techniques of control.

In contrast to a society with natural fertility, a society that desires to limit fertility and has the means to do so may use those means to delay child-bearing, space child-bearing, or stop child-bearing. Delaying sexual intercourse (or marriage), or the adoption of natural or artificial means of contraception are most often an individual or family decision, not a matter of a state policy or societal-wide sanctions. On the other hand, individuals who assume some sense of control over their own fertility can also accelerate the frequency or success of child-bearing through planning.

At the societal level, declining fertility is almost an inevitable result of growing secular education of women. The exercise of moderate to high levels of fertility control does not necessarily imply low fertility rates. Even among societies that exercise substantial fertility control, societies with an equal *ability* to exercise fertility control (to determine how many children to have and when to bear them) may display widely different *levels* of fertility (numbers of children borne) associated with individual and cultural preferences for the number of children or size of families.

In contrast to *fertility control,* which is mainly an individual-level decision, governments may attempt to exercise *population control* by increasing access to means of contraception or by other population policies and programmes. The idea of "population control" as a governmental or societal-level regulation of population growth does not require 'fertility control' in the sense that it has been defined above, since a state can affect the growth of a society's population even if that society practices little fertility control. It's also important to embrace policies favoring population *increase* as an aspect of population control, and not to assume that states want to control population only by limiting its growth.

To stimulate population growth, governments may support not only immigration but also pronatalist policies such as tax benefits, financial awards, paid work leaves, and childcare to encourage the bearing of additional children. Such policies have been pursued in recent years in France and Sweden, for example. With the same goal of increasing population growth, on occasion governments have sought to limit the use of abortion or modern means of birth control. An example was Romania under Nicolae Ceausescu in 1966 banning access to contraception and abortion on demand.

In ecology, population control is on occasions considered to be done solely by predators, diseases, parasites, and environmental factors. In a constant environment, population control is regulated by the availability of food, water, and safety. The maximum number of a species or individuals that can be supported in a certain area is called the carrying capacity. At many times human effects on animal and plant populations are also considered. Migrations of animals may be seen as a natural way of population control, for the food on land is more abundant on some seasons. The area of the migrations' start is left to reproduce the food supply for large mass of animals next time around.

India is an interesting example of changes in government measures to control the country's population. The Indian government, concerned that the rapidly growing population would adversely affect economic growth and living standards implemented an official family planning programme in the late 1950s and early 1960s; it was the first country in the world to do so. Later extreme policies backfired with writers such as Salman Rushdie's Midnight Children lambasting forced sterilisation of petty convicts and incentivised sterilisation during the Indian Emergency. Later, policitians and press reports named Sanjay Gandhi as the policy's governmental head.

In Animals

Animal population control is the practice of intentionally altering the size of any animal population besides humans. It may involve culling, translocation, or manipulation of the animal's reproduction. The growth of animal population may be limited by environmental factors such as food supply or predation. The main Biotic Factors that effect population growth include:

- ***Food***— both the quantity and the quality of food are important. Snails, for example, cannot reproduce successfully in an environment low in calcium, no matter how much food there is, because they need this mineral for shell growth.
- ***Predators***— as a prey population becomes larger, it becomes easier for predators to find prey. If the number of predators suddenly falls, the prey species might increase in number extremely quickly.
- ***Competitors***— other organisms may require the same resources from the environment, and so reduce growth of a population.For example all plants compete for light. Competition for territory and for mates can drastically reduce the growth of individual organisms.
- ***Parasites***— These may cause disease, and slow down the growth and reproductive rate of organisms within a population.

Important Abiotic factors affecting population growth include:

- ***Temperature***— Higher temperatures speed up enzyme-catalyzed reactions and increase growth.
- ***Oxygen availability***— affects the rate of energy production by respiration.
- ***Light availability***— for photosynthesis. light may also control breeding cycles in animals and plants.
- ***Toxins and pollutants***— tissue growth can be reduced by the presence of, for example, sulphur dioxide, and reproductive success may be affected by pollutants such as estrogen like substances.

Species

In biology, a species is one of the basic units of biological classification and a taxonomic rank. A species is often defined as a group of organisms capable of interbreeding and producing fertile offspring. While in many cases this definition is adequate, more precise or differing measures are often used, such as similarity of DNA, morphology or ecological niche. Presence of specific locally adapted traits may further subdivide species into subspecies.

The commonly used names for plant and animal taxa sometimes correspond to species: for example, 'lion', 'walrus', and 'Camphor tree' — each refers to a species. In other cases common names do not: for example, 'deer' refers to a family of 34 species, including Eld's Deer, Red Deer and Elk (Wapiti). The last two species were once considered a single species, illustrating how species boundaries may change with increased scientific knowledge.

Each species is placed within a single genus. This is a hypothesis that the species is more closely related to other species within its genus than to species of other genera. All species are given a binomial name consisting of the generic name and specific name (or specific epithet). For example, *Boa constrictor*, which is commonly called by its bionomial name, and is one of five species of the *Boa* genus.

A usable definition of the word 'species' and reliable methods of identifying particular species are essential for stating and testing biological theories and for measuring biodiversity. Traditionally, multiple examples of a proposed species must be studied for unifying characters before it can be regarded as a species. Extinct species known only from fossils are generally difficult to give precise taxonomic rankings to.

Because of the difficulties with both defining and tallying the total numbers of different species in the world, it is estimated that there are anywhere between 2 and 100 million different species.

Biologists' Working Definition

A usable definition of the word 'species' and reliable methods of identifying particular species is essential for stating and testing biological theories and for measuring biodiversity. Traditionally, multiple examples of a proposed species must be studied for unifying characters before it can be regarded as a species. It is generally difficult to give precise taxonomic rankings to extinct species known only from fossils.

Some biologists may view species as statistical phenomena, as opposed to the traditional idea, with a species seen as a class of organisms. In that case, a species is defined as a separately evolving lineage that forms a single gene pool. Although properties such as DNA-sequences and morphology are used to help separate closely related lineages, this definition has fuzzy boundaries. However, the exact definition of the term 'species' is still controversial, particularly in prokaryotes, and this is called the species problem. Biologists have proposed a range of more precise definitions, but the definition used is a pragmatic choice that depends on the particularities of the species concerned.

Placement within Generation

Ideally, a species is given a formal, scientific name, although in practice there are very many unnamed species (which have only been described, not named). When a species is named, it is placed within a genus. From a scientific point of view this can be regarded as a hypothesis that the species is more closely related to other species within its genus (if any) than to species of other genera. Species and genus are usually defined as part of a larger taxonomic hierarchy. The best-known taxonomic ranks are, in order: life, domain, kingdom, phylum, class, order, family, genus, and species. This assignment to a genus is not immutable; later a different (or the same) taxonomist may assign it to a different genus, in which case the name will also change.

In biological nomenclature, the name for a species is a two-part name (a binomial name), treated as Latin, although roots from any language can be used as well as names of locales or individuals. The generic name is listed first (with its leading letter capitalized), followed by a second term, the specific name (or specific epithet). For example, the species commonly known as the Longleaf Pine is *Pinus palustris*; gray wolves belong to the species *Canis lupus*, coyotes to *Canis latrans*, golden jackals to *Canis aureus*, etc., and all of those belong to the genus *Canis* (which also contains many other species). The name of the species is the whole binomial, not just the second term (which may be called the specific name for animals).

This binomial naming convention, later formalized in the biological codes of nomenclature, was first used by Leonhart Fuchs and introduced as the standard by Carolus Linnaeus in his 1753, *Species Plantarum* (followed by his, 1758 *Systema Naturae*, 10th edition). At that time, the chief biological theory was that species represented independent acts of creation by God and were therefore considered objectively real and immutable, so the hypothesis of common descent did not apply.

Abbreviated Names

Books and articles sometimes intentionally do not identify species fully and use the abbreviation *'sp.'* in the singular or *'spp.'* in the plural in place of the specific epithet: for example, *Canis* sp. This commonly occurs in the following types of situations:

- The authors are confident that some individuals belong to a particular genus but are not sure to which exact species they belong. This is particularly common in paleontology.
- The authors use 'spp.' as a short way of saying that something applies to many species within a genus, but do not wish to say that it applies to all species within that genus. If scientists mean that something applies to all species within a genus, they use the genus name without the specific epithet.

In books and articles, genus and species names are usually printed in italics. If using 'sp.' and 'spp.', these should not be italicized.

It is surprisingly difficult to define the word 'species' in a way that applies to all naturally occurring organisms, and the debate among biologists about how to define 'species' and how to identify actual species is called the species problem. Over two dozen distinct definitions of 'species' are in use amongst biologists.

Most textbooks follow Ernst Mayr's definition of a species as "groups of actually or potentially interbreeding natural populations, which are reproductively isolated from other such groups".

Various parts of this definition serve to exclude some unusual or artificial matings:

- Those that occur only in captivity (when the animal's normal mating partners may not be available) or as a result of deliberate human action.
- Animals that may be physically and physiologically capable of mating but, for various reasons, do not normally do so in the wild.

The typical textbook definition above works well for most multi-celled organisms, but there are several types of situations in which it breaks down:

- By definition it applies only to organisms that reproduce sexually. So it does not work for asexually reproducing single-celled organisms and for the relatively few parthenogenetic multi-celled organisms. The term 'phylotype' is often applied to such organisms.
- Biologists frequently do not know whether two morphologically similar groups of organisms are 'potentially' capable of interbreeding.
- There is considerable variation in the degree to which hybridization may succeed under natural conditions, or even in the degree to which some organisms use sexual reproduction between individuals to breed.
- In ring species, members of adjacent populations interbreed successfully but members of some non-adjacent populations do not.

- In a few cases it may be physically impossible for animals that are members of the same species to mate. However, these are cases in which human intervention has caused gross morphological changes, and are therefore excluded by the biological species concept.

Horizontal gene transfer makes it even more difficult to define the word 'species'. There is strong evidence of horizontal gene transfer between very dissimilar groups of prokaryotes, and at least occasionally between dissimilar groups of eukaryotes; and Williamson argues that there is evidence for it in some crustaceans and echinoderms. All definitions of the word 'species' assume that an organism gets all its genes from one or two parents that are very like that organism, but horizontal gene transfer makes that assumption false.

Definitions of Species

The question of how best to define 'species' is one that has occupied biologists for centuries, and the debate itself has become known as the species problem. Darwin wrote in chapter II of on the origin of species.

No one definition has satisfied all naturalists; yet every naturalist knows vaguely what he means when he speaks of a species. Generally the term includes the unknown element of a distinct act of creation.

But later, in *The Descent of Man*, when addressing "The question whether mankind consists of one or several species", Darwin revised his opinion to say:

- It is a hopeless endeavour to decide this point on sound grounds, until some definition of the term 'species' is generally accepted; and the definition must not include an element that cannot possibly be ascertained, such as an act of creation.

The modern theory of evolution depends on a fundamental redefinition of 'species'. Prior to Darwin, naturalists viewed species as ideal or general types, which could be exemplified by an ideal specimen bearing all the traits general to the species. Darwin's theories shifted attention from uniformity to variation and from the general to the particular. According to intellectual historian Louis Menand.

Once our attention is redirected to the individual, we need another way of making generalizations. We are no longer interested in the conformity of an individual to an ideal type; we are now interested in the relation of an individual to the other individuals with which it interacts. To generalize about groups of interacting individuals, we need to drop the language of types and essences, which is prescriptive (telling us what finches should be), and adopt the language of statistics and probability, which is predictive (telling us what the average finch, under specified conditions, is likely to do). Relations will be more important than categories; functions, which are variable, will be more important than purposes; transitions will be more important than boundaries; sequences will be more important than hierarchies.

This shift results in a new approach to 'species'; Darwin concluded that species are what they appear to be: ideas, which are provisionally useful for naming groups of interacting individuals. "I look at the term species", he wrote, "as one arbitrarily given for the sake of convenience to a set of individuals closely resembling each other ... It does not essentially differ from the word variety, which is given to less distinct and more fluctuating forms. The term variety, again, in comparison with mere individual differences, is also applied arbitrarily, and for convenience sake".

Practically, biologists define species as *populations of organisms that have a high level of genetic similarity*. This may reflect an adaptation to the same niche, and the transfer of genetic material from one individual to others, through a variety of possible means. The exact level of similarity used in such a definition is arbitrary, but this is the most common definition used for organisms that reproduce asexually (asexual reproduction), such as some plants and microorganisms.

This lack of any clear species concept in microbiology has led to some authors arguing that the term 'species' is not useful when studying bacterial evolution. Instead they see genes as moving freely between even distantly related bacteria, with the entire bacterial domain being a single gene pool. Nevertheless, a kind of rule of thumb has been established, saying that species of *Bacteria* or *Archaea* with 16S rRNA gene sequences more similar than 97 per cent to each other need to be checked by DNA-DNA Hybridization if they belong to the same species or not. This concept has been updated recently, saying that the border of 97 per cent was too low and can be raised to 98.7 per cent.

In the study of sexually reproducing organisms, where genetic material is shared through the process of reproduction, the ability of two organisms to interbreed and produce fertile offspring of both sexes is generally accepted as a simple indicator that the organisms share enough genes to be considered members of the same species. Thus a 'species' is a group of interbreeding organisms.

This definition can be extended to say that a species is a group of organisms that could potentially interbreed — fish could still be classed as the same species even if they live in different lakes, as long as they could still interbreed were they ever to come into contact with each other. On the other hand, there are many examples of series of three or more distinct populations, where individuals of the population in the middle can interbreed with the populations to either side, but individuals of the populations on either side cannot interbreed. Thus, one could argue that these populations constitute a single species, or two distinct species. This is not a paradox; it is evidence that species are defined by gene frequencies, and thus have fuzzy boundaries.

Consequently, any single, universal definition of 'species' is necessarily arbitrary. Instead, biologists have proposed a range of definitions; which definition a biologists uses is a pragmatic choice, depending on the particularities of that biologist's research.

Typological Species

A group of organisms in which individuals are members of the species if they sufficiently conform to certain fixed properties or 'rights of passage'. The clusters of variations or phenotypes within specimens (i.e. longer or shorter tails) would differentiate the species. This method was used as a 'classical' method of determining species, such as with Linnaeus early in evolutionary theory. However, we now know that different phenotypes do not always constitute different species (e.g.: a 4-winged Drosophila born to a 2-winged mother is not a different species). Species named in this manner are called *morphospecies*.

Morphological Species

A population or group of populations that differs morphologically from other populations. For example, we can distinguish between a chicken and a duck because they have different shaped bills and the duck has webbed feet. Species have been defined in this way since well before the beginning of recorded history. This species concept is highly criticized because more recent genetic data reveal that genetically distinct populations may look very similar and, contrarily, large morphological differences sometimes exist between very closely related populations. Nonetheless, most species known have been described solely from morphology.

Biological/Isolation Species

A set of actually or potentially interbreeding populations. This is generally a useful formulation for scientists working with living examples of the higher taxa like mammals, fish, and birds, but more problematic for organisms that do not reproduce sexually. The results of breeding experiments done in artificial conditions may or may not reflect what would happen if the same organisms encountered each other in the wild, making it difficult to gauge whether or not the results of such experiments are meaningful in reference to natural populations.

Biological/Reproductive Species

Two organisms that are able to reproduce naturally to produce fertile offspring of both sexes. Organisms that can reproduce but almost always make infertile hybrids of at least one sex, such as a mule, hinny or F1 male cattalo are not considered to be the same species.

Recognition Species

Based on shared reproductive systems, including mating behaviour. The Recognition concept of species has been introduced by Hugh E. H. Paterson.

Mate-recognition Species

A group of organisms that are known to recognize one another as potential mates. Like the isolation species concept above, it applies only to organisms that reproduce sexually. Unlike the isolation species concept, it focuses specifically on pre-mating reproductive isolation.

Evolutionary/Darwinian Species

A group of organisms that shares an ancestor; a lineage that maintains its integrity with respect to other lineages through both time and space. At some point in the progress of such a group, some members may diverge from the main population and evolve into a subspecies, a process that eventually will lead to the formation of a new full species if isolation (geographical or ecological) is maintained.

Phylogenetic

A group of organisms that shares an ancestor; a lineage that maintains its integrity with respect to other lineages through both time and space. At some point in the progress of such a group, members may diverge from one another: when such a divergence becomes sufficiently clear, the two populations are regarded as separate species. This differs from evolutionary species in that the parent species goes extinct taxonomically when a new species evolve, the mother and daughter populations now forming two new species. Subspecies as such are not recognized under this approach; either a population is a phylogenetic species or it is not taxonomically distinguishable.

Ecological Species

A set of organisms adapted to a particular set of resources, called a niche, in the environment. According to this concept, populations form the discrete phonetic clusters that we recognize as species because the ecological and evolutionary processes controlling how resources are divided up tend to produce those clusters.

Genetic Species

Based on similarity of DNA of individuals or populations. Techniques to compare similarity of DNA include DNA-DNA hybridization, and genetic fingerprinting (or DNA barcoding).

PHENETIC SPECIES (BASED ON PHENOTYPES)

Micro Species

Species that reproduce without meiosis or fertilization so that each generation is genetically identical to the previous generation.

Cohesion Species

Most inclusive population of individuals having the potential for phenotypic cohesion through intrinsic cohesion mechanisms. This is an expansion of the mate-recognition species concept to allow for post-mating isolation mechanisms; no matter whether populations can hybridize successfully, they are still distinct cohesion species if the amount of hybridization is insufficient to completely mix their respective gene pools.

Evolutionarily Significant Unit (ESU)

An evolutionarily significant unit is a population of organisms that is considered distinct for purposes of conservation. Often referred to as a species or a *wildlife species*, an ESU also has several possible definitions, which coincide with definitions of species.

In practice, these definitions often coincide, and the differences between them are more a matter of emphasis than of outright contradiction. Nevertheless, no species concept yet proposed is entirely objective, or can be applied in all cases without resorting to judgment. Given the complexity of life, some have argued that such an objective definition is in all likelihood impossible, and biologists should settle for the most practical definition.

For most vertebrates, this is the biological species concept (BSC), and to a lesser extent (or for different purposes) the phylogenetic species concept (PSC). Many BSC subspecies are considered species under the PSC; the difference between the BSC and the PSC can be summed up insofar as that the BSC defines a species as a consequence of manifest evolutionary *history*, while the PSC defines a species as a consequence of manifest evolutionary *potential*. Thus, a PSC species is 'made' as soon as an evolutionary lineage has started to separate, while a BSC species starts to exist only when the lineage separation is complete. Accordingly, there can be considerable conflict between alternative classifications based upon the PSC versus BSC, as they differ completely in their treatment of taxa that would be considered subspecies under the latter model (e.g., the numerous subspecies of honey bees).

The naming of a particular species may be regarded as a *hypothesis* about the evolutionary relationships and distinguishability of that group of organisms. As further information comes to hand, the hypothesis may be confirmed or refuted. Sometimes, especially in the past when communication was more difficult, taxonomists working in isolation have given two distinct names to individual organisms later identified as the same species. When two named species are discovered to be of the same species, the older species name is usually retained, and the newer species name dropped, a process called *synonymization*, or colloquially, as lumping. Dividing a taxon into multiple, often new, taxons is called splitting. Taxonomists are often referred to as 'lumpers' or 'splitters' by their colleagues, depending on their personal approach to recognizing differences or commonalities between organisms.

Traditionally, researchers relied on observations of anatomical differences, and on observations of whether different populations were able to interbreed successfully, to distinguish species; both anatomy and breeding behaviour are still important to assigning species status. As a result of the revolutionary (and still ongoing) advance in microbiological research techniques, including DNA analysis, in the last few decades, a great deal of additional knowledge about the differences and similarities between species has become available. Many populations formerly regarded as separate species are now considered a single taxon, and many formerly grouped populations have been split. Any taxonomic level (species, genus, family, etc.) can be synonymized or split, and at higher taxonomic levels, these revisions have been still more profound.

From a taxonomical point of view, groups within a species can be defined as being of a taxon hierarchically lower than a species. In zoology only the subspecies is used, while in botany the variety, subvariety, and form are used as well. In conservation biology, the concept of evolutionary significant units (ESU) is used, which may be define either species or smaller distinct population segments. Identifying and naming species is the providence of alpha taxonomy.

In the earliest works of science, a species was simply an individual organism that represented a group of similar or nearly identical organisms. No other relationships beyond that group were implied. Aristotle used the words *genus* and *species* to mean generic and specific categories. Aristotle and other pre-Darwinian scientists took the species to be distinct and unchanging, with an 'essence', like the chemical elements. When early observers began to develop systems of organization for living things, they began to place formerly isolated species into a context. Many of these early delineation schemes would now be considered whimsical and these included consanguinity based on color (all plants with yellow flowers) or behaviour (snakes, scorpions and certain biting ants).

In the 18th century Swedish scientist Carolus Linnaeus classified organisms according to differences in the form of reproductive apparatus. Although his system of classification sorts organisms according to degrees of similarity, it made no claims about the relationship between similar species. At that time, it was still widely believed that there was no organic connection between species, no matter how similar they appeared. This approach also suggested a type of idealism: the notion that each species existed as an 'ideal form'. Although there are always differences (although sometimes minute) between individual organisms, Linnaeus considered such variation problematic. He strove to identify individual organisms that were exemplary of the species, and considered other non-exemplary organisms to be deviant and imperfect.

By the 19th century most naturalists understood that species could change form over time, and that the history of the planet provided enough time for major changes. Jean-Baptiste Lamarck, in his 1809 *Zoological Philosophy*, offered one of the first logical arguments against creationism. The new emphasis was on determining *how* a species could change over time. Lamarck suggested that an organism could pass on an acquired trait to its offspring, i.e., the giraffe's long neck was attributed to generations of giraffes stretching to reach the leaves of higher treetops (this well-known and simplistic example, however, does not do justice to the breadth and subtlety of Lamarck's ideas). With the acceptance of the natural selection idea of Charles Darwin in the 1860s, however, Lamarck's view of goal-oriented evolution, also known as a teleological process, was eclipsed. Recent interest in inheritance of acquired characteristics centres around epigenetic processes, e.g. methylation, that do not affect DNA sequences, but instead alter expression in an inheritable manner. Thus, neo-lamarckism, as it is sometimes termed, is not a challenge to the theory of evolution by natural selection.

Charles Darwin and Alfred Wallace provided what scientists now consider as the most powerful and compelling theory of evolution. Darwin argued that it was populations that evolved, not individuals. His argument relied on a radical shift in perspective from that of Linnaeus: rather than defining species in ideal terms (and searching for an ideal representative and rejecting deviations), Darwin considered variation among individuals to be natural. He further argued that variation, far from being problematic, actually provides the *explanation* for the existence of distinct species.

Darwin's work drew on Thomas Malthus' insight that the rate of growth of a biological population will always outpace the rate of growth of the resources in the environment, such as the food supply. As a result, Darwin argued, not all the members of a population will be able to survive and reproduce. Those that did will, on average, be the ones possessing variations—

however slight—that make them slightly better adapted to the environment. If these variable traits are heritable, then the offspring of the survivors will also possess them. Thus, over many generations, adaptive variations will accumulate in the population, while counter-adaptive traits will tend to be eliminated.

It should be emphasized that whether a variation is adaptive or non-adaptive depends on the environment: different environments favour different traits. Since the environment effectively selects which organisms live to reproduce, it is the environment (the 'fight for existence') that selects the traits to be passed on. This is the theory of evolution by natural selection. In this model, the length of a giraffe's neck would be explained by positing that proto-giraffes with longer necks would have had a significant reproductive advantage to those with shorter necks. Over many generations, the entire population would be a species of long-necked animals.

In 1859, when Darwin published his theory of natural selection, the mechanism behind the inheritance of individual traits was unknown. Although Darwin made some speculations on how traits are inherited (pangenesis), his theory relies only on the fact that inheritable traits *exist*, and are variable (which makes his accomplishment even more remarkable.) Although Gregor Mendel's paper on genetics was published in 1866, its significance was not recognized. It was not until 1900 that his work was rediscovered by Hugo de Vries, Carl Correns and Erich vön Tschermak, who realised that the 'inheritable traits' in Darwin's theory are genes.

The theory of the evolution of species through natural selection has two important implications for discussions of species—consequences that fundamentally challenge the assumptions behind Linnaeus' taxonomy. First, it suggests that species are not just similar, they may actually be related. Some students of Darwin argue that *all* species are descended from a common ancestor. Second, it supposes that 'species' are not homogeneous, fixed, permanent things; members of a species are all different, and over time species change. This suggests that species do not have any clear boundaries but are rather momentary statistical effects of constantly changing gene-frequencies. One may still use Linnaeus' taxonomy to identify individual plants and animals, but one can no longer think of species as independent and immutable.

The rise of a new species from a parental line is called speciation. There is no clear line demarcating the ancestral species from the descendant species.

Although the current scientific understanding of species suggests that there is no rigorous and comprehensive way to distinguish between different species in *all* cases, biologists continue to seek concrete ways to operationalize the idea. One of the most popular biological definitions of species is in terms of reproductive isolation; if two creatures cannot reproduce to produce fertile offspring of both sexes, then they are in different species. This definition captures a number of intuitive species boundaries, but it remains imperfect. It has nothing to say about species that reproduce asexually, for example, and it is very difficult to apply to extinct species. Moreover, boundaries between species are often fuzzy: there are examples where members of one population can produce fertile offspring of both sexes with a second population, and members of the second population can produce fertile offspring of both sexes with members of a third population, but members of the first and third population cannot produce fertile offspring, or can only produce fertile offspring of the homozygous sex. Consequently, some people reject this definition of a species.

Richard Dawkins defines two organisms as conspecific if and only if they have the same number of chromosomes and, for each chromosome, both organisms have the same number of nucleotides. However, most if not all taxonomists would strongly disagree. For example, in many amphibians, most notably in New Zealand's *Leiopelma* frogs, the genome consists of 'core' chromosomes that are mostly invariable and accessory chromosomes, of which exist a number of possible combinations. Even though the chromosome numbers are highly variable between populations, these can interbreed successfully and form a single evolutionary unit. In plants, polyploidy is extremely commonplace with few restrictions on interbreeding; as individuals with an odd number of chromosome sets are usually sterile, depending on the actual number of chromosome sets present, this results in the odd situation where some individuals of the same evolutionary unit can interbreed with certain others and some cannot, with all populations being eventually linked as to form a common gene pool.

The classification of species has been profoundly affected by technological advances that have allowed researchers to determine relatedness based on molecular markers, starting with the comparatively crude blood plasma precipitation assays in the mid-20th century to Charles Sibley's ground-breaking DNA-DNA hybridization studies in the 1970s leading to DNA sequencing techniques. The results of these techniques caused revolutionary changes in the higher taxonomic categories (such as phyla and classes), resulting in the reordering of many branches of the phylogenetic tree . For taxonomic categories below genera, the results have been mixed so far; the pace of evolutionary change on the molecular level is rather slow, yielding clear differences only after considerable periods of reproductive separation. DNA-DNA hybridization results have led to misleading conclusions, the Pomarine Skua — Great Skua phenomenon being a famous example. Turtles have been determined to evolve with just one-eighth of the speed of other reptiles on the molecular level, and the rate of molecular evolution in albatrosses is half of what is found in the rather closely related storm-petrels. The hybridization technique is now obsolete and is replaced by more reliable computational approaches for sequence comparison. Molecular taxonomy is not directly based on the evolutionary processes, but rather on the overall change brought upon by these processes. The processes that lead to the generation and maintenance of variation such as mutation, crossover and selection are not uniform (see also molecular clock). DNA is only extremely rarely a direct target of natural selection rather than changes in the DNA sequence enduring over generations being a result of the latter; for example, silent transition-transversion combinations would alter the melting point of the DNA sequence, but not the sequence of the encoded proteins and thus are a possible example where, for example in microorganisms, a mutation confers a change in fitness all by itself.

CHAPTER 3

Metapopulation

A metapopulation consists of a group of spatially separated populations of the same species which interact at some level. The term metapopulation was coined by Richard Levins in 1970 to describe a model of population dynamics of insect pests in agricultural fields, but the idea has been most broadly applied to species in naturally or artificially fragmented habitats. In Levins' own words, it consists of 'a population of populations'.

A metapopulation is generally considered to consist of several distinct populations together with areas of suitable habitat which are currently unoccupied. In classical metapopulation theory, each population cycles in relative independence of the other populations and eventually goes extinct as a consequence of demographic stochasticity (fluctuations in population size due to random demographic events); the smaller the population, the more prone it is to extinction.

Although individual populations have finite life-spans, the metapopulation as a whole is often stable because immigrants from one population (which may, for example, be experiencing a population boom) are likely to re-colonize habitat which has been left open by the extinction of another population. They may also emigrate to a small population and rescue that population from extinction (called the *rescue effect*).

The development of metapopulation theory, in conjunction with the development of source-sink dynamics, emphasised the importance of connectivity between seemingly isolated populations. Although no single population may be able to guarantee the long-term survival of a given species, the combined effect of many populations may be able to do this.

Metapopulation theory was first developed for terrestrial ecosystems, and subsequently applied to the marine realm. In fisheries science, the term 'sub-population' is equivalent to the metapopulation science term 'local population'. Most marine examples are provided by relatively sedentary species occupying discrete patches of habitat, with both local recruitment and recruitment from other local populations in the larger metapopulation. Kritzer & Sale have argued against strict application of the metapopulation definitional criteria that extinction risks to local populations must be non-negligible.

Predation and Oscillations

The first experiments with predation and spatial heterogeneity were conducted by G.F. Gause in the 1930's, based on the Lotka-Volterra equation, which was formulated in the mid-1920s, but no further application had been conducted. The Lotka-Volterra equation suggested that the relationship between predators and their prey would result in population oscillations over time based on the initial densities of predator and prey. Gause's early experiments to prove the predicted oscillations of this theory failed because the predator-prey interactions were not influenced by immigration. However, once immigration was introduced, the population cycles accurately depicted the oscillations predicted by the Lotka-Volterra equation, with the peaks in prey abundance shifted slightly to the left of the peaks of the predator densities. Huffaker's experiments expanded on those of Gause by examining how both the factors of migration and spatial heterogeneity lead to predator-prey oscillations.

Huffaker's Experiments on Predator-prey Interactions

In order to study predation and population oscillations, Huffaker used mite species, one being the predator and the other being the prey. He set up a controlled experiment using oranges, which the prey fed on, as the spatially structured habitat in which the predator and prey would interact. At first, Huffaker experienced difficulties similar to those of Gause in creating a stable predator-prey interaction. By using oranges only, the prey species quickly went extinct followed consequently with predator extinction. However, he discovered that by modifying the spatial structure of the habitat, he could manipulate the population dynamics and allow the overall survival rate for both species to increase. He did this by altering the distance between the prey and oranges (their food), establishing barriers to predator movement, and creating corridors for the prey to disperse. These changes resulted in increased habitat patches and in turn provided more areas for the prey to seek temporary protection. When the prey would go extinct locally at one habitat patch, they were able to re-establish by migrating to new patches before being attacked by predators. This habitat spatial structure of patches allowed for coexistence between the predator and prey species and promoted a stable population oscillation model. Although the term metapopulation had not yet been coined, the environmental factors of spatial heterogeneity and habitat patchiness would later describe the conditions of a metapopulation relating to how groups of spatially separated populations of species interact with one another. Huffaker's experiment is significant because it showed how metapopulations can directly affect the predator-prey interactions and in turn influence population dynamics.

Huffaker's studies of spatial structure and species interactions are an example of early experimentation in metapopulation dynamics. Since the experiments of Huffaker and Levins , models have been created which integrate stochastic factors. These models have proven that the combination of environmental variability (stochascity) and relatively small migration rates cause indefinite or unpredictable persistence. However, Huffaker's experiment almost guaranteed infinite persistence because of the controlled immigration variable.

Stochastic Patch Occupancy Models (SPOMs)

One major drawback of the Levins model is that it is deterministic, whereas the fundamental metapopulation processes are stochastic. Metapopulations are particularly useful when discussing species in disturbed habitats, and the viability of their populations, i.e., how likely they are to become extinct in a given time interval. The Levins model cannot address this issue. A simple way to extend the Levins' model to incorporate space and stochastic considerations is by using the contact process (mathematics). Simple modifications to this model can also incorporate for patch dynamics. At a given percolation threshold, habitat fragmentation effects take place in these configuration predicting more drastic extinction thresholds.

For conservation biology purposes, metapopulation models must include:

(*a*) the finite nature of metapopulations (how many patches are suitable for habitat), and

(*b*) the probabilistic nature of extinction and colonisation.

Also, note that in order to apply these models, the extinctions and colonisations of the patches must be asynchronous.

Micro Habitat Patches (MHPs) and Bacterial Metapopulations

By combining nanotechnology with landscape ecology, a habitat landscape can be nanofabricated on-chip by building a collection of nanofabricated bacterial habitats, and connecting them by corridors in different topological arrangements and with nano-scale channels providing them with the local ecosystem service of habitat renewal. These landscapes of MHPs can be used as physical implementations of an adaptive landscape by generating an spatial mosaic of patches of opportunity distributed in space and time. The patchy nature of these fluidic landscapes allows for the study of adapting bacterial cells in a metapopulation system operating on-chip within a synthetic ecosystem. The metapopulation biology and evolutionary ecology of these bacterial systems, in these synthetic ecosystems, can be addressed using experimental biophysics.

Habitat Fragmentation

Habitat fragmentation as the name implies, describes the emergence of discontinuities (fragmentation) in an organism's preferred environment (habitat). Habitat fragmentation can be caused by geological processes that slowly alter the layout of the physical environment or by human activity such as land conversion, which can alter the environment on a much faster time scale. The former is suspected of being one of the major causes of speciation. The latter is causative in extinctions of many species.

Habitat fragmentation is frequently caused by humans when native vegetation is cleared for human activities such as agriculture, rural development, urbanization and the creation of hydroelectric reservoirs. Habitats which were once continuous become divided into separate fragments. After intensive clearing, the separate fragments tend to be very small islands isolated from each other by crop land, pasture, pavement, or even barren land. The latter is often the result of slash and burn farming in tropical forests. In the wheatbelt of central western New South Wales, Australia 90 per cent of the native vegetation has been cleared and over 99 per cent of the tallgrass prairie of North America has been cleared, resulting in extreme habitat fragmentation.

The term habitat fragmentation includes five discrete phenomena:

- Reduction in the total area of the habitat
- Decrease of the interior : edge ratio
- Isolation of one habitat fragment from other areas of habitat
- Breaking up of one patch of habitat into several smaller patches
- Decrease in the average size of each patch of habitat

One of the major ways that habitat fragmentation affects biodiversity is by reduction in the amount of available habitat (such as rainforests, boreal forests, oceans, marshlands, etc.) for all organisms in an ecological niche. Habitat fragmentation invariably involves some amount of habitat destruction. Plants and other sessile organisms in these areas are usually directly destroyed. Mobile animals (especially birds and mammals) retreat into remnant patches of habitat. This can lead to crowding effects and increased competition.

The remaining habitat fragments are smaller than the original habitat. Species that can move between fragments may use more than one fragment. Species which cannot move between fragments must make do with what is available in the single fragment in which they ended up. Since one of the major causes of habitat destruction is agricultural development, habitat fragments are rarely representative samples of the initial landscape.

Area is the primary determinant of the number of species in a fragment. The size of the fragment will influence the number of species which are present when the fragment was initially created, and will influence the ability of these species to persist in the fragment. Small fragments of habitat can only support small populations of plants and animals and small populations are more vulnerable to extinction. Minor fluctuations in climate, resources, or other factors that would be unremarkable and quickly corrected in large populations can be catastrophic in small, isolated populations. Thus fragmentation of habitat is an important cause of species extinction. Population dynamics of subdivided populations tend to vary asynchronously. In an unfragmented landscape a declining population can be 'rescued' by immigration from a nearby expanding population. In fragmented landscapes, the distance between fragments may prevent this from happening. Additionally, unoccupied fragments of habitat that are separated from a source of immigrants by some barrier are less likely to be repopulated than adjoining fragments. Even small species such as the Columbia spotted frog are reliant on the rescue effect. Studies showed 25 per cent of juveniles travel a distance over 200m compared to 4 per cent of adults. Of these, 95 per cent remain in their new locale, demonstrating that this journey is necessary for survival. It rains a lot in the high dispersal in other amphibians indicate that it is crucial to the endangerment of rare species in the class.

Additionally, habitat fragmentation leads to edge effects. Microclimactic changes in light, temperature and wind can alter the ecology around the fragment, and in the interior and exterior portions of the fragment. Fires become more likely in the area as humidity drops and temperature and wind levels rise. Exotic and pest species may establish themselves easily in such disturbed environments, and the proximity of domestic animals often upsets the natural ecology. Also, habitat along the edge of a fragment has a different climate and favours different species from the interior habitat. Small fragments are therefore unfavourable for species which require interior habitat.

Habitat fragmentation is often a cause of species becoming threatened or endangered. The existence of viable habitat is critical to the survival of any species, and in many cases the fragmentation of any remaining habitat can lead to difficult decisions for conservation biologists. Given a limited amount of resources available for conservation is it preferable to protect the existing isolated patches of habitat or to buy back land to get the largest possible continuous piece of land? This ongoing debate is often referred to as SLOSS (Single Large or Several Small).

One solution to the problem of habitat fragmentation is to link the fragments by preserving or planting corridors of native vegetation. This has the potential to mitigate the problem of isolation but not the loss of interior habitat. In rare cases a Conservation reliant species may gain some measure of disease protection by being distributed in isolated habitats.

Another mitigation measure is the enlargement of small remnants in order to increase the amount of interior habitat. This may be impractical since developed land is often more expensive and could require significant time and effort to restore.

The best solution is generally dependent on the particular species or ecosystem that is being considered. More mobile species, like most birds, do not need connected habitat while some smaller animals, like rodents, may be more exposed to predation in open land. These questions generally fall under the headings of metapopulations island biogeography.

Chapter 4
Speciation

Speciation is the evolutionary process by which new biological species arise. The biologist Orator F. Cook seems to have been the first to coin the term 'speciation' for the splitting of lineages or 'cladogenesis', as opposed to 'anagenesis' or 'phyletic evolution' occurring within lineages. Whether genetic drift is a minor or major contributor to speciation is the subject of much ongoing discussion. There are four geographic modes of speciation in nature, based on the extent to which speciating populations are geographically isolated from one another: allopatric, peripatric, parapatric, and sympatric. Speciation may also be induced artificially, through animal husbandry or laboratory experiments. Observed examples of each kind of speciation are provided throughout.

All forms of natural speciation have taken place over the course of evolution; however it still remains a subject of debate as to the relative importance of each mechanism in driving biodiversity.

One example of natural speciation is the diversity of the three-spined stickleback, a marine fish that, after the last ice age, has undergone speciation into new freshwater colonies in isolated lakes and streams. Over an estimated 10,000 generations, the sticklebacks show structural differences that are greater than those seen between different genera of fish including variations in fins, changes in the number or size of their bony plates, variable jaw structure, and colour differences.

There is debate as to the rate at which speciation events occur over geologic time. While some evolutionary biologists claim that speciation events have remained relatively constant over time, some palaeontologists such as Niles Eldredge and Stephen Jay Gould have argued that species usually remain unchanged over long stretches of time, and that speciation occurs only over relatively brief intervals, a view known as *punctuated equilibrium*.

During allopatric (from the ancient Greek *allos*, 'other' + Greek *patra*, 'fatherland') speciation, a population splits into two geographically isolated populations (for example, by habitat fragmentation due to geographical change such as mountain building or social change such as emigration). The isolated populations then undergo genotypic and/or phenotypic divergence as:

(*a*) they become subjected to dissimilar selective pressures;

(*b*) they independently undergo genetic drift;

(*c*) different mutations arise in the two populations.

When the populations come back into contact, they have evolved such that they are reproductively isolated and are no longer capable of exchanging genes.

Observed Instances

Island genetics, the tendency of small, isolated genetic pools to produce unusual traits, has been observed in many circumstances, including insular dwarfism and the radical changes among certain famous island chains, for example on Komodo. The Galápagos islands are particularly famous for their influence on Charles Darwin. During his five weeks there he heard that Galápagos tortoises could be identified by island, and noticed that Mockingbirds differed from one island to another, but it was only nine months later that he reflected that such facts could show that species were changeable. When he returned to England, his speculation on evolution deepened after experts informed him that these were separate species, not just varieties, and famously that other differing Galápagos birds were all species of finches. Though the finches were less important for Darwin, more recent research has shown the birds now known as Darwin's finches to be a classic case of adaptive evolutionary radiation.

Peripatric

In peripatric speciation, a subform of allopatric speciation, new species are formed in isolated, smaller peripheral populations that are prevented from exchanging genes with the main population. It is related to the concept of a founder effect, since small populations often undergo bottlenecks. Genetic drift is often proposed to play a significant role in peripatric speciation.

Observed Instances

- Mayr bird fauna
- The Australian bird *Petroica multicolor*
- Reproductive isolation occurs in populations of *Drosophila* subject to population bottlenecking.

The London Underground mosquito is a variant of the mosquito *Culex pipiens* that entered in the London Underground in the nineteenth century. Evidence for its speciation include genetic divergence, behavioural differences, and difficulty in mating.

Parapatric

In parapatric speciation, there is only partial separation of the zones of two diverging populations afforded by geography; individuals of each species may come in contact or cross habitats from time to time, but reduced fitness of the heterozygote leads to selection for behaviours or mechanisms that prevent their inter-breeding. Parapatric speciation is modelled on continuous variation within a 'single', connected habitat acting as a source of natural selection rather than the effects of isolation of habitats produced in peripatric and allopatric speciation.

Ecologists refer to parapatric and peripatric speciation in terms of ecological niches. A niche must be available in order for a new species to be successful.

- Ring species
- The *Larus* gulls form a ring species around the North Pole.
- The *Ensatina* salamanders, which form a ring round the Central Valley in California.
- The Greenish Warbler (*Phylloscopus trochiloides*), around the Himalayas.
- The grass *Anthoxanthum* has been known to undergo parapatric speciation in such cases as mine contamination of an area.

Sympatric speciation refers to the formation of two or more descendant species from a single ancestral species all occupying the same geographic location.

In sympatric speciation, species diverge while inhabiting the same place. Often-cited examples of sympatric speciation are found in insects that become dependent on different host plants in the same area. However, the existence of sympatric speciation as a mechanism of speciation is still hotly contested. People have argued that the evidences of sympatric speciation are in fact examples of micro-allopatric, or heteropatric speciation. The most widely accepted example of sympatric speciation is that of the cichlids of Lake Nabugabo in East Africa, which is thought to be due to sexual selection.

Until recently, there has a been a dearth of hard evidence that supports this form of speciation, with a general feeling that interbreeding would soon eliminate any genetic differences that might appear. But there has been at least one recent study that suggests that sympatric speciation has occurred in Tennessee cave salamanders.

The three-spined sticklebacks, freshwater fishes, that have been studied by Dolph Schluter (who received his Ph.D. for his work on Darwin's finches with Peter J. Grant) and his current colleagues in British Columbia, were once thought to provide an intriguing example best explained by sympatric speciation. Schluter and colleagues found:

- Two different species of three-spined sticklebacks in each of five different lakes
- A large benthic species with a large mouth that feeds on large prey in the littoral zone.
- a smaller limnetic species — with a smaller mouth — that feeds on the small plankton in open water.
- DNA analysis indicates that each lake was colonized independently, presumably by a marine ancestor, after the last ice age.
- DNA analysis also shows that the two species in each lake are more closely related to each other than they are to any of the species in the other lakes.
- The two species in each lake are reproductively isolated; neither mates with the other.
- The benthic species from one lake will spawn with the benthic species from the other lakes; and
- Likewise the limnetic species from the different lakes will spawn with each other.
- These benthic and limnetic species even display their mating preferences when presented with sticklebacks from Japanese lakes; that is, a Canadian benthic prefers a Japanese benthic over its close limnetic cousin from its own lake.
- Their conclusion: in each lake, what began as a single population faced such competition for limited resources that:
    - ❑ disruptive selection – competition favoring fishes at either extreme of body size and mouth size over those nearer the mean – coupled with:
        - — assortative mating —each size preferred mates like it — favored a divergence into two subpopulations exploiting different food in different parts of the lake.

— The fact that this pattern of speciation occurred the same way on three separate occasions suggests strongly that ecological factors in a sympatric population can cause speciation.

However, the DNA evidence cited above is from mitochondrial DNA (mtDNA), which can often move easily between closely related species ('introgression') when they hybridize. A more recent study, using genetic markers from the nuclear genome, shows that limnetic forms in different lakes are more closely related to each other (and to marine lineages) than to benthic forms in the same lake. The three-spine stickleback is now usually considered an example of 'double invasion' (a form of allopatric speciation) in which repeated invasions of marine forms have subsequently differentiated into benthic and limnetic forms. The three-spine stickleback provides an example of how molecular biogeographic studies that rely solely on mtDNA can be misleading, and that consideration of the genealogical history of alleles from multiple unlinked markers (i.e. nuclear genes) is necessary to infer speciation histories.

Sympatric speciation driven by ecological factors may also account for the extraordinary diversity of crustaceans living in the depths of Siberia's Lake Baikal.

Speciation via Polyploidization

Polyploidy is a mechanism often attributed to causing some speciation events in sympatry. Not all polyploids are reproductively isolated from their parental plants, so an increase in chromosome number may not result in the complete cessation of gene flow between the incipient polyploids and their parental diploids.

Polyploidy is observed in many species of both plants and animals, and results in rapid speciation since offspring of, for example, tetraploid x diploid matings result in triploid sterile progeny. It has been proposed that many of the existing plant and most animal species have undergone an event of polyploidization in their evolutionary history. However, reproduction is often by parthenogenesis since polyploid animals are often sterile. [needs further editing—not true in plants. Rare instances of polyploid mammals are known, but most often result in prenatal death.

Hawthorn Fly

One example of evolution at work is the case of the hawthorn fly, *Rhagoletis pomonella*, also known as the apple maggot fly, which appears to be undergoing sympatric speciation. Different populations of hawthorn fly feed on different fruits. A distinct population emerged in North America in the 19th century some time after apples, a non-native species, were introduced.

This apple-feeding population normally feeds only on apples and not on the historically preferred fruit of hawthorns. The current hawthorn feeding population does not normally feed on apples. Some evidence, such as the fact that six out of thirteen allozyme loci are different, that hawthorn flies mature later in the season and take longer to mature than apple flies; and that there is little evidence of interbreeding (researchers have documented a 4-6 per cent hybridization rate) suggests that sympatric speciation is occurring. The emergence of the new hawthorn fly is an example of evolution in progress.

Reinforcement (Wallace Effect)

Reinforcement is the process by which natural selection increases reproductive isolation. It may occur after two populations of the same species are separated and then come back into contact. If their reproductive isolation was complete, then they will have already developed into two separate incompatible species. If their reproductive isolation is incomplete, then further mating between the populations will produce hybrids, which may or may not be fertile. If the hybrids are infertile, or fertile but less fit than their ancestors, then there will be no further reproductive isolation and speciation has essentially occurred (e.g., as in horses and donkeys.) The reasoning behind this is that if the parents of the hybrid offspring each have naturally selected traits for their own certain environments, the hybrid offspring will bear traits from both, therefore would not fit either ecological niche as well as either parent. The low fitness of the hybrids would cause selection to favour assortative mating, which would control hybridization. This is sometimes called the Wallace effect after the evolutionary biologist Alfred Russel Wallace who suggested in the late 19th century that it might be an important factor in speciation. If the hybrid offspring are more fit than their ancestors, then the populations will merge back into the same species within the area they are in contact.

Reinforcement is required for both parapatric and sympatric speciation. Without reinforcement, the geographic area of contact between different forms of the same species, called their 'hybrid zone', will not develop into a boundary between the different species. Hybrid zones are regions where diverged populations meet and interbreed. Hybrid offspring are very common in these regions, which are usually created by diverged species coming into secondary contact. Without reinforcement the two species would have uncontrollable inbreeding. Reinforcement may be induced in artificial selection experiments as described below.

Artificial Speciation

New species have been created by domesticated animal husbandry, but the initial dates and methods of the initiation of such species are not clear.

For example, domestic sheep were created by hybridisation, and no longer produce viable offspring with *Ovis orientalis*, one species from which they are descended. Domestic cattle, on the other hand, can be considered the same species as several varieties of wild ox, gaur, yak, etc., as they readily produce fertile offspring with them.

The best-documented creations of new species in the laboratory were performed in the late 1980s. William Rice and G.W. Salt bred fruit flies, *Drosophila melanogaster*, using a maze with three different choices of habitat such as light/dark and wet/dry. Each generation was placed into the maze, and the groups of flies that came out of two of the eight exits were set apart to breed with each other in their respective groups. After thirty-five generations, the two groups and their offspring were isolated reproductively because of their strong habitat preferences: they mated only within the areas they preferred, and so did not mate with flies that preferred the other areas. The history of such attempts is described in Rice and Hostert

Hybrid Speciation

Hybridization between two different species sometimes leads to a distinct phenotype. This phenotype can also be fitter than the parental lineage and as such natural selection may then favor these individuals. Eventually, if reproductive isolation is achieved, it may lead to a separate species. However, reproductive isolation between hybrids and their parents is particularly difficult to achieve and thus hybrid speciation is considered an extremely rare event. The Mariana Mallard is known to have arisen from hybrid speciation.

Hybridization without change in chromosome number is called homoploid hybrid speciation. It is considered very rare but has been shown in *Heliconius* butterflies and sunflowers. Polyploid speciation, which involves changes in chromosome number, is a more common phenomenon, especially in plant species.

Gene Transposition as a Cause

Theodosius Dobzhansky, who studied fruit flies in the early days of genetic research in 1930s, speculated that parts of chromosomes that switch from one location to another might cause a species to split into two different species. He mapped out how it might be possible for sections of chromosomes to relocate themselves in a genome. Those mobile sections can cause sterility in inter-species hybrids, which can act as a speciation pressure. In theory, his idea was sound, but scientists long debated whether it actually happened in nature. Eventually a competing theory involving the gradual accumulation of mutations was shown to occur in nature so often that geneticists largely dismissed the moving gene hypothesis.

However, 2006 research shows that jumping of a gene from one chromosome to another can contribute to the birth of new species. This validates the reproductive isolation mechanism, a key component of speciation.

Interspersed repetitive DNA sequences function as isolating mechanisms. These repeats protect newly evolving gene sequences from being overwritten by gene conversion, due to the creation of non-homologies between otherwise homologous DNA sequences. The non-homologies create barriers to gene conversion. This barrier allows nascent novel genes to evolve without being overwritten by the progenitors of these genes. This uncoupling allows the evolution of new genes, both within gene families and also allelic forms of a gene. The importance is that this allows the splitting of a gene pool without requiring physical isolation of the organisms harbouring those gene sequences.

Humans have genetic similarities with chimpanzees and gorillas, suggesting common ancestors. Analysis of genetic drift and recombination using a Markov model suggests humans and chimpanzees speciated apart 4.1 million years ago.

CHAPTER 5
Carrying Capacity

The carrying capacity of a biological species in an environment is the population size of the species that the environment can sustain indefinitely, given the food, habitat, water and other necessities available in the environment. In population biology, carrying capacity is defined as the environment's maximal load, which is different from the concept of population equilibrium.

For the human population, more complex variables such as sanitation and medical care are sometimes considered as part of the necessary establishment. As population density increases, birth rate often decreases and death rate typically increases. The difference between the birth rate and the death rate is the 'natural increase'. The carrying capacity could support a positive natural increase, or could require a negative natural increase. Thus, the carrying capacity is the number of individuals an environment can support without significant negative impacts to the given organism and its environment. Below carrying capacity, populations typically increase, while above, they typically decrease. A factor that keeps population size at equilibrium is known as a regulating factor. Population size decreases above carrying capacity due to a range of factors depending on the species concerned, but can include insufficient space, food supply, or sunlight. The carrying capacity of an environment may vary for different species and may change over time due to a variety of factors, including: food availability, water supply, environmental conditions and living space.

The origins of the term carrying capacity are uncertain with researchers variously stating that it was used 'in the context of international shipping' or that it was first used during 19th Century laboratory experiments with micro-organisms. A recent review finds the first use of the term in an 1845 report by the US Secretary of State to the Senate.

It is possible for a species to exceed its carrying capacity temporarily. Population could then crash. Population variance occurs as part of the natural selection process but may occur more dramatically in some instances. Due to a variety of factors, one determinant of carrying capacity may lag behind another. For example, a waste product of a species may build up to toxic levels slower than the food supply is exhausted. The result is a fluctuation in the population around the equilibrium point which is statistically significant. These fluctuations are increases or decreases in the population until either the population returns to the original equilibrium point, or a new equilibrium is established. These fluctuations may be more devastating for an ecosystem than are gradual population corrections, because, if they produce drastic decreases or increases, those may affect other species in the ecosystem and they may begin to move with statistical significance around their own equilibrium points. The fear is of a domino-like effect, where the final consequences are unknown and may lead to collapses of species or even whole ecosystems.

Examples

One of the world's best-studied predator-prey relationships is the moose and wolf population of Isle Royale National Park in Lake Superior. Without the wolves, the moose would overgraze the island's vegetation. Without the moose, the wolves would die. The first scientists who studied the issue thought that the wolves would eventually overpopulate and kill all the moose calves, then die from famine . This has not occurred as inbreeding, disease and environmental factors have limited the wolf population naturally.

Easter Island has been cited as an example of a human population crash. When fewer than 100 humans first arrived, the island was covered with trees with a large variety of food types. In 1722, the island was visited by Jacob Roggeveen, who estimated a population of 2000 to 3000 inhabitants with very few trees, 'a rich soil, good climate' and 'all the county was under cultivation'. Half a century later, it was described as 'a poor land' and 'largely uncultivated'. The ecological collapse which followed has been variously attributed to overpopulation, slave traders, European diseases (including a smallpox epidemic which killed so many so quickly, the dead were left unburied and a tuberculosis epidemic which wiped out a quarter of the population), social upheaval and invasive species (such as the Polynesian rats which may have wiped out the ground nesting birds and eaten the palm tree seeds). Whatever the combination of factors, only 111 inhabitants were left on the island in 1877. For whatever reasons (whether Moai worship, survival, status or sheer ignorance), the question of how many humans the island could realistically support never seems to have been answered. This example, and others, are discussed at length in Jared Diamond's *Collapse* and subsequent literature.

The Chincoteague Pony Swim is a human-assisted example.

Both herds are managed differently. The National Park Service owns and manages the Maryland herd while the Chincoteague Volunteer Fire Company owns and manages the Virginia herd. The Virginia herd, referred to as the 'Chincoteague' ponies, is allowed to graze on Chincoteague National Wildlife Refuge, through a special use permit issued by the U.S. Fish and Wildlife Service. The size of both herds is restricted to approximately 150 adult animals each in order to protect the other natural resources of the wildlife refuge.

A further example is the Island of Tarawa, where the finite amount of space is evident, especially since landfills cannot be dug to dispose of solid waste, due to constraints in the subsurface rock and lack of topographic elevations. With colonial influence and an abundance of food (relative to life before the year 1850), the population has expanded to the extent that overpopulation is transparently present.

Mathematics

The Lotka-Volterra equations are simple mathematical model of population dynamics which show how in a closed system, like that of the wolves and moose on Isle Royale, limited prey will cause the predator population to decline rapidly. An extended example can be used where multiple species are competing for the same resources, or single species feed on multiple prey.

Humans

In the words of one researcher: "Over the past three decades, many scholars have offered detailed critiques of carrying capacity–particularly its formal application–by pointing out that the term does not successfully capture the multi-layered processes of the human-environment link, and that it often has a blame-the-victim framework. These scholars most often cite the fluidity and non-equilibrium nature of this relationship, and the role of external forces in influencing environmental change, as key problems with the term".

In other words, the relationship of humans to their environment may be more complex than is the relationship of other species to theirs. Humans can alter the type and degree of their impact on their environment by, for instance, increasing the productivity of land through more intensive farming techniques, leaving a defined local area, or scaling back their consumption; of course, humans may also irreversibly decrease the productivity of the environment or increase consumption.

Supporters of the concept argue that humans, like every species, have a finite carrying capacity. Animal population size, living standards, and resource depletion vary, but the concept of carrying capacity still applies. The World3 model of Donella Meadows deals with carrying capacity at its core.

Carrying capacity, at its most basic level, is about organisms and food supply, where 'X' amount of humans need 'Y' amount of food to survive. If the humans neither gain or lose weight in the long run, the calculation is fairly accurate. If the quantity of food is invariably equal to the 'Y' amount, carrying capacity has been reached. Humans, with the need to enhance their reproductive success (see Richard Dawkins' *The Selfish Gene*, understand that food supply can vary and also that other factors in the environment can alter humans' need for food. A house, for example, might mean that one does not need to eat as much to stay warm as one otherwise would. Over time, monetary transactions have replaced barter and local production, and consequently modified local human carrying capacity. However, purchases also impact regions thousands of miles away.

One way to estimate human demand compared to ecosystem's carrying capacity is 'Ecological Footprint' accounting. Rather than speculating about future possibilities and limitations imposed by carrying capacity constraints, Ecological Footprint accounting provides empirical, non-speculative assessments of the past. It compares historically regeneration rates (biocapacity) against historical human demand (Ecological Footprint) in the same year. One result shows that humanity's demand for 1999 exceeded the planet's biocapacity for 1999 by over 20 per cent. This overshoot can be maintained for some time since stocks can be liquidated (e.g., overfishing, deforestation) and sinks can be filled up (e.g., carbon accumulation in the atmosphere). Countries can have Footprints that are higher than their biocapacity for three reasons, they can:

(a) net-import;

(b) net-emit CO_2 to other countries; and

(c) overshoot their own ecosystems.

But for the world as a whole only overshoot is available, since there is no trade with other planets.

Carrying capacity debates focusing on the possibility or impossibility of future technological break-throughs for substituting resources raise the question of whether or not it is possible to define a measure of carrying capacity or sustainability which does not already contain implicit assumptions about solutions to the problems of resource over-exploitation and environmental degradation.

Possible Reduction of Earth's Carrying Capacity in the 21st Century

Agricultural capability on Earth expanded in the last quarter of the 20th century. But now there are many projections of a continuation of the decline in world agricultural capability (and hence carrying capacity) which began in the 1990s. Most conspicuously, China's food production is forecast to decline by 37 per cent by the last half of the 21st century, placing a strain on the entire carrying capacity of the world, as China's population could expand to about 1.5 billion people by the year 2050. This reduction in China's agricultural capability (as in other world regions) is largely due to the world water crisis and especially due to mining groundwater beyond sustainable yield, which has been happening in China since the mid-20th century.

The process of defining Tourism Carrying Capacity (TCC) is composed of two parts. It follows (in principle) the conceptual framework for TCC as described by Shelby and Heberlein (1986), and these parts are described as follows:

- Descriptive part (A): Describes how the system (tourist destination) under study works, including physical, ecological, social, political and economic aspects of tourist development. Within this context of particular importance is the identification of:
  - *Constraints:* limiting factors that cannot be easily managed. They are inflexible, in the sense that the application of organisational, planning, and management approaches, or the development of appropriate infrastructure does not alter the thresholds associated with such constraints.
  - *Bottlenecks:* limiting factors of the system which managers can manipulate (number of visitors at a particular place).
  - *Impacts:* elements of the system affected by the intensity and type of use. The type of impact determines the type of capacity (ecological-physical, social, etc.). Emphasis should be placed on significant impacts.
- *Evaluative part (B):* Describes how an area should be managed and the level of acceptable environmental impacts. This part of the process starts with the identification (if it does not already exist) of the desirable condition or preferable type of development. Within this context, goals and management objectives need to be defined, alternative fields of actions evaluated and a strategy for tourist development formulated. On the basis of this, Tourism Carrying Capacity can be defined. Within this context, of particular importance is the identification of:
  - Goals and/or objectives: (i.e. to define the type of experience or other outcomes which a recreational setting should provide).

Differing Definitions

First of all, the carrying capacity can be the motivation to attract tourists visit the destination. The tourism industry, especially in national parks and protected areas, is subject to the concept of carrying capacity so as to determine the scale of tourist activities which can be sustained at specific times in different places. Various scholar over the years have developed several arguments developed about the definition of carrying capacity. Middleton and Hawkins defined carrying capacity as a measure of the tolerance of a site or building which is open to tourist activities, and the limit beyond which an area may suffer from the adverse impacts of tourism. Chamberlain defined it as the level of human activity which an area can accommodate without either it deteriorating, the resident community being adversely affected or the quality of visitors' experience declining. Clark defined carrying capacity as a certain threshold (level) of tourism activity, beyond which there will be damage to the environment and its natural inhabitants.

The World Tourism Organisation argues that carrying capacity is the maximum number of people who may visit a tourist destination at the same time, without causing destruction of the physical, economic and socio-cultural environment and/or an unacceptable decrease in the quality of visitors' satisfaction. In the publication, 'Agenda 21 for the Travel and Tourism Venture: towards environmentally sustainable development', the Secretary-General of the World Tourism Organization.

The definitions of carrying capacity need to be considered as processes within a planning process for tourism development which involves:

- Setting capacity limits for sustaining tourism activities in an area. This involves a vision about local development and decisions about managing tourism.
- Overall measuring of tourism carrying capacity does not have to lead to a single number, like the number of visitors.
- In addition, carrying capacity may contain various limits in respect to the three components (physical-ecological, socio-demographic and political-economic).

"Carrying capacity is not just a scientific concept or formula of obtaining a number beyond which development should cease, but a process where the eventual limits must be considered as guidance. They should be carefully assessed and monitored, complemented with other standards, etc. Carrying capacity is not fixed. It develops with time and the growth of tourism and can be affected by management techniques and controls".

The reason for considering carrying capacity as a process, rather than a means of protection of various areas is in spite of the fact that carrying capacity was once a guiding concept in recreation and tourism management literature.

Because of its conceptual elusiveness, lack of management utility and inconsistent effectiveness in minimising visitors' impacts, carrying capacity has been largely re-conceptualized into management by objectives approaches, namely: the limits of acceptable change (LAC), and the visitor experience and resource protection (VERP) as the two planning and management decision-making processes based on the new understanding of carrying capacity. These two have been deemed more appropriate in the tourism planning processes of protected areas, especially in the United States, and have over the years been adapted and modified for use in sustainable tourism and ecotourism contexts.

Ecological Footprint

The ecological footprint is a measure of human demand on the Earth's ecosystems. It compares human demand with planet Earth's ecological capacity to regenerate. It represents the amount of biologically productive land and sea area needed to regenerate the resources a human population consumes and to absorb and render harmless the corresponding waste. Using this assessment, it is possible to estimate how much of the Earth (or how many planet Earths) it would take to support humanity if everybody lived a given lifestyle. For 2006, humanity's total ecological footprint was estimated at 1.4 planet Earths — in other words, humanity uses ecological services 1.4 times as fast as Earth can renew them. Every year, this number is recalculated — with a three year lag due to the time it takes for the UN to collect and publish all the underlying statistics.

While the term *'ecological footprint'* is widely used, methods of measurement vary. However, calculation standards are now emerging to make results more comparable and consistent.

The first academic publication about the ecological footprint was by William Rees in 1992. The ecological footprint concept and calculation method was developed as the PhD dissertation of Mathis Wackernagel, under Rees' supervision at the University of British Columbia in Vancouver, Canada, from 1990-1994. Originally, Wackernagel and Rees called the concept 'appropriated carrying capacity'. To make the idea more accessible, Rees came up with the term 'ecological footprint', inspired by a computer technician who praised his new computer's 'small footprint on the desk'. In early 1996, Wackernagel and Rees published the book *'Our Ecological Footprint: Reducing Human Impact on the Earth'*.

Ecological footprint analysis compares human demand on nature with the biosphere's ability to regenerate resources and provide services. It does this by assessing the biologically productive land and marine area required to produce the resources a population consumes and absorb the corresponding waste, using prevailing technology. Footprint values at the end of a survey are categorized for Carbon, Food, Housing, and Goods and Services as well as the total footprint number of Earths needed to sustain the world's population at that level of consumption. This approach can also be applied to an activity such as the manufacturing of a product or driving of a car. This resource accounting is similar to life cycle analysis wherein the consumption of energy, biomass (food, fiber), building material, water and other resources are converted into a normalized measure of land area called 'global hectares' (*gha*).

Per capita ecological footprint (EF) is a means of comparing consumption and lifestyles, and checking this against nature's ability to provide for this consumption. The tool can inform policy by examining to what extent a nation uses more (or less) than is available within its territory, or to what extent the nation's lifestyle would be replicable worldwide. The footprint can also be a useful tool to educate people about carrying capacity and over-consumption, with the aim of altering personal behaviour. Ecological footprints may be used to argue that many current lifestyles are not sustainable. Such a global comparison also clearly shows the inequalities of resource use on this planet at the beginning of the twenty-first century.

In 2006, the average biologically productive area per person worldwide was approximately 1.8 global hectares (gha) per capita. The U.S. footprint per capita was 9.0 gha, and that of Switzerland was 5.6 gha per person, while China's was 1.8 gha per person. The WWF claims that the human footprint has exceeded the biocapacity (the available supply of natural resources) of the planet by 20 per cent. Wackernagel and Rees originally estimated that the available biological capacity for the 6 billion people on Earth at that time was about 1.3 hectares per person, which is smaller than the 1.8 global hectares published for 2006, because the initial studies neither used global hectares nor included bioproductive marine areas.

Ecological footprinting is now widely used around the globe as an indicator of environmental sustainability. It can be used to measure and manage the use of resources throughout the economy. It can be used to explore the sustainability of individual lifestyles, goods and services, organizations, industry sectors, neighborhoods, cities, regions and nations. Since 2006, a first set of ecological footprint standards exist that detail both communication and calculation procedures.

Methodology

The ecological footprint accounting method at the national level is described in the Living Planet Report or in more detail in Global Footprint Network's. The national accounts committee of Global Footprint Network has also published a research agenda on how the method will be improved.

There have been differences in the methodology used by various ecological footprint studies. Examples include how sea area should be counted, how to account for fossil fuels, how to account for nuclear power (many studies simply consider it to have the same ecological footprint as fossil fuels), which data sources used, when average global numbers or local numbers should be used when looking at a specific area, how space for biodiversity should be included, and how imports/exports should be accounted for. However, with the new footprint standards, the methods are converging.

In 2003, Jason Venetoulis, PhD, Carl Mas, Christopher Gudoet, Dahlia Chazan, and John Talberth -a team of researchers at Redefining- developed Footprint 2.0. Footprint 2.0 offers a series of theoretical and methodological improvements to the standard footprint approach. The primary advancements were to include the entire surface of the Earth in biocapacity estimates, allocate space for other (non-human) species, change the basis of equivalence factors from agricultural land to net primary productivity (NPP), and change the carbon component of the footprint, based on global carbon models. The advancements were peer reviewed and published in several books, and have been well received by teachers, researchers, and advocacy organizations concerned about the ecological implications of humanity's footprint.

Studies in the United Kingdom

The UK's average ecological footprint is 5.45 global hectares per capita (gha) with variations between regions ranging from 4.80 gha (Wales) to 5.56 gha (East England). Two recent studies have examined relatively low-impact small communities. BedZED, a 96-home mixed-income housing development in South London, was designed by Bill Dunster Architects and sustainability consultants BioRegional for the Peabody Trust. Despite being populated by relatively 'mainstream' home-buyers, BedZED was found to have a footprint of 3.20 gha due to on-site renewable energy production, energy-efficient architecture, and an extensive green lifestyles programme that included on-site London's first carsharing club. The report did not measure the added footprint of the 15,000 visitors who have toured BedZED since its completion in 2002. Findhorn Ecovillage, a rural intentional community in Moray, Scotland, had a total footprint of 2.56 gha, including both the many guests and visitors who travel to the community to undertake residential courses there and the nearby campus of Cluny Hill College. However, the residents alone have a footprint of 2.71 gha, a little over half the UK national average and one of the lowest ecological footprints of any community measured so far in the industrialized world Keveral Farm, an organic farming community in Cornwall, was found to have a footprint of 2.4 gha, though with substantial differences in footprints among community members.

Early criticism was published by van den Bergh and Verbruggen in 1999; another criticism was published in 2008. A more complete review commissioned by the Directorate-General for the Environment (European Commission) and published in June 2008 provides the most updated independent assessment of the method. A number of countries have engaged in research collaborations to test the validity of the method. This includes Switzerland, Germany, United Arab Emirates, and Belgium.

Grazi et al. (2007) have performed a systematic comparison of the ecological footprint method with spatial welfare analysis that includes environmental externalities, agglomeration effects and trade advantages. They find that the two methods can lead to very distinct, and even opposite, rankings of different spatial patterns of economic activity. However, this should not be surprising, since the two methods address different research questions.

Calculating the ecological footprint for densely populated areas, such as a city or small country with a comparatively large population — e.g. New York and Singapore respectively — may lead to the perception of these populations as 'parasitic'. This is because these communities have little intrinsic biocapacity, and instead must rely upon large *hinterlands*. Critics argue that this is a dubious characterization since mechanized rural farmers in developed nations may easily consume more resources than urban inhabitants, due to transportation requirements and the unavailability of economies of scale. Furthermore, such moral conclusions seem to be an argument for autarky. Some even take this train of thought a step further, claiming that the Footprint denies the benefits of trade. Therefore, the critics argue that that the Footprint can only be applied globally.

The method seems to reward the replacement of original ecosystems with high-productivity agricultural monocultures by assigning a higher biocapacity to such regions. For example, replacing ancient woodlands or tropical forests with monoculture forests or plantations may improve the ecological footprint. Similarly, if organic farming yields were lower than those of conventional methods, this could result in the former being 'penalized' with a larger ecological footprint. Of course, this insight, while valid, stems from the idea of using the footprint as one's only metric. If the use of ecological footprints are complemented with other indicators, such as one for biodiversity, the problem could maybe be solved. Indeed, WWF's Living Planet Report complements the biennial Footprint calculations with the Living Planet Index of biodiversity. Manfred Lenzen and Shauna Murray have created a modified Ecological Footprint that takes biodiversity into account for use in Australia.

Although the ecological footprint model prior to 2008 treated nuclear power in the same manner as coal power, the actual real world effects of the two are radically different. A life cycle analysis centered around the Swedish Forsmark Nuclear Power Plant estimated carbon dioxide emissions at 3.10 g/kWh and 5.05 g/kWh in 2002 for the Torness Nuclear Power Station.

This compares to 11 g/kWh for hydroelectric power, 950 g/kWh for installed coal, 900 g/kWh for oil and 600 g/kWh for natural gas generation in the United States in 1999.

The Swedish utility Vattenfall did a study of full life cycle emissions of Nuclear, Hydro, Coal, Gas, Solar Cell, Peat and Wind which the utility uses to produce electricity.

The net result of the study was that nuclear power produced 3.3 grams of carbon dioxide per KW-Hr of produced power. This compares to 400 for natural gas and 700 for coal (according to this study). The study also concluded that nuclear power produced the smallest amount of CO_2 of any of their electricity sources.

Claims exist that the problems of nuclear waste do not come anywhere close to approaching the problems of fossil fuel waste. A 2004 article from the BBC states: "The World Health Organization (WHO) says 3 million people are killed worldwide by outdoor air pollution annually from vehicles and industrial emissions, and 1.6 million indoors through using solid fuel." In the U.S. alone, fossil fuel waste kills 20,000 people each year. A coal power plant releases 100 times as much radiation as a nuclear power plant of the same wattage.

It is estimated that during 1982, US coal burning released 155 times as much radioactivity into the atmosphere as the Three Mile Island incident. In addition, fossil fuel waste causes global warming, which leads to increased deaths from hurricanes, flooding, and other weather events. The World Nuclear Association provides a comparison of deaths due to accidents among different forms of energy production. In their comparison, deaths per TW-yr of electricity produced (in UK and USA) from 1970 to 1992 are quoted as 885 for hydropower, 342 for coal, 85 for natural gas, and 8 for nuclear.

CHAPTER 6

Overpopulation

Overpopulation is a condition where an organism's numbers exceed the carrying capacity of its habitat. The term often refers to the relationship between the human population and its environment, the Earth. Steve Jones, head of the biology department at University College London, has said, "Humans are 10,000 times more common than we should be, according to the rules of the animal kingdom, and we have agriculture to thank for that. Without farming, the world population would probably have reached half a million by now." The world's population has significantly increased in the last 50 years, mainly due to medical advancements and substantial increases in agricultural productivity.

The recent rapid increase in human population over the past two centuries has raised concerns that humans are beginning to overpopulate the Earth, and that the planet may not be able to sustain present or larger numbers of inhabitants. The population has been growing continuously since the end of the Black Death, around the year 1400; at the beginning of the 19th century, it had reached roughly 1,000,000,000 (1 billion). Increases in life expectancy and resource availability during the industrial and green revolutions led to rapid population growth on a worldwide level. By 1960, the world population had reached 3 billion; it doubled to 6 billion over the next four decades. As of 2009, the estimated annual growth rate was 1.10 per cent, down from a peak of 2.2 per cent in 1963, and the world population stood at roughly 6.7 billion. Current projections show a steady decline in the population growth rate, with the population expected to reach between 8 and 10.5 billion between the year 2040 and 2050.

The scientific consensus is that the current population expansion and accompanying increase in usage of resources is linked to threats to the ecosystem. The InterAcademy Panel Statement on Population Growth, which was ratified by 58 member national academies in 1994, called the growth in human numbers 'unprecedented', and stated that many environmental problems, such as rising levels of atmospheric carbon dioxide, global warming, and pollution, were aggravated by the population expansion. At the time, the world population stood at 5.5 billion, and optimistic scenarios predicted a peak of 7.8 billion by 2050, a number that current estimates show will be reached around 2030.

Overpopulation does not depend only on the size or density of the population, but on the ratio of population to available sustainable resources. It also depends on the way resources are used and distributed throughout the population. Overpopulation can result from an increase in births, a decline in mortality rates due to medical advances, from an increase in immigration, or from an unsustainable biome and depletion of resources. It is possible for very sparsely populated areas to be overpopulated, as the area in question may have a meager or non-existent capability to sustain human life (e.g. a desert).

The resources to be considered when evaluating whether an ecological niche is overpopulated include clean water, clean air, food, shelter, warmth, and other resources necessary to sustain life. If the quality of human life is addressed, there may be additional resources considered, such as medical care, education, proper sewage treatment and waste disposal. Overpopulation places competitive stress on the basic life sustaining resources, leading to a diminished quality of life.

History of Concern

Concern about overpopulation is relatively recent in origin. Throughout history, populations have grown slowly despite high birth rates, due to the population-reducing effects of war, plagues and high infant mortality. During the 750 years before the Industrial Revolution, the world's population hardly increased, remaining under 250 million.

By the beginning of the 19th century, the world population had grown to a billion individuals, and intellectuals such as Thomas Malthus and physiocratic economists predicted that mankind would outgrow its available resources, since a finite amount of land was incapable of supporting an endlessly increasing population. Mercantillists argued that a large population was a form of wealth, which made it possible to create bigger markets and armies.

The human population has gone through a number of periods of growth since the dawn of civilization in the Holocene period, around 10,000 BC. The beginning of civilization coincides with the final receding of glacial ice following the end of the last glacial period. It is estimated that about 1,000,000 people, subsisting on hunting and foraging, inhabited the Earth in the period before the neolithic revolution, when human activity shifted away from hunter-gathering and towards very primitive farming.

Around 8,000 BC, at the dawn of agriculture, the population of the world was approximately 5 million. The next several millennia saw minimal changes in the population, with a steady growth beginning in 1,000 BCE, plateauing (or alternatively, peaking) in 1 BCE, at between 200 and 300 million people.

The Plague of Justinian caused Europe's population to drop by around 50 per cent between 541 and the 8th century. Steady growth resumed in 800 CE. This growth was disrupted by frequent plagues; most notably, the Black Death during the 14th century. the effects of the Black Death are thought to have reduced the world's population, then at an estimated 450 million, to between 350 and 375 million by 1400. The population of Europe stood at over 70 million in 1340; these levels did not return until 200 years later.

On the other side of the globe, China's population at the founding of the Ming dynasty in 1368 stood close to 60 million, approaching 150 million by the end of the dynasty in 1644.

England's population reached an estimated 5.6 million in 1650, up from an estimated 2.6 million in 1500 New crops that had come to Asia and Europe from the Americas via the Spanish colonizers in the 16th century contributed to the population growth.

Since being introduced by Portuguese traders in the 16th century, maize and manioc have replaced traditional African crops as the continent's most important staple food crops.

Alfred W. Crosby speculated that increased production of maize, manioc, and other American crops "... enabled the slave traders drew many, perhaps most, of their cargoes from the rain forest areas, *precisely* those areas where American crops enabled heavier settlement than before".

The population of the Americas in 1500 may have been between 50 and 100 million.

Encounters between European explorers and populations in the rest of the world often introduced local epidemics of extraordinary virulence. Archaeological evidence indicates that the death of around 90 per cent of the Native American population of the New World was caused by Old World diseases such as smallpox, measles, and influenza.

Over the centuries, the Europeans had developed high degrees of immunity to these diseases, while the indigenous peoples had no such immunity.

After the effects of the plagues had subsided during the 17th century, shortly before the Industrial Revolution, the world population began to grow once again. In parts of Asia, like China, the population doubled from 60 to 150 million.

After the start of the Industrial Revolution, during the 18th century, the rate of population growth began to increase. By the end of the century, the world's population was estimated at just under 1 billion.

At the turn of the 20th century, the world's population was roughly 1.6 billion. By 1940, this figure had increased to 2.3 billion.

Dramatic growth beginning in 1950 (above 1.8% per year) coincided with greatly increased food production as a result of the industrialisation of agriculture brought about by the Green Revolution The rate of growth peaked in 1964, at about 2.2 per cent per year.

The world population is currently estimated to be 6,880,300,000, with unreported variability.

1900

- Africa — 133 million
- Asia — 946 million
- Europe — 408 million
- Latin America & Caribbean — 74 million
- North America — 82 million

Projections of Population Growth

According to projections, the world population will continue to grow until at least 2050, with the population reaching 9 billion in 2040, and some predictions putting the population in 2050 as high as 11 billion.

According to the United Nations' World Population Prospects report:

- The world population is currently growing by approximately 74 million people per year. Current United Nations predictions estimate that the world population will reach 9.0 billion around 2050, assuming a decrease in average fertility rate from 2.5 down to 2.0.
- Almost all growth will take place in the less developed regions, where today's 5.3 billion population of underdeveloped countries is expected to increase to 7.8 billion in 2050. By contrast, the population of the more developed regions will remain mostly unchanged, at 1.2 billion. An exception is the United States population, which is expected to increase 44 per cent from 305 million in 2008 to 439 million in 2050.

- In 2000-2005, the average world fertility was 2.65 children per woman, about half the level in 1950-1955 (5 children per woman). In the medium variant, global fertility is projected to decline further to 2.05 children per woman.
- During 2005-2050, nine countries are expected to account for half of the world's projected population increase: India, Pakistan, Nigeria, Democratic Republic of the Congo, Bangladesh, Uganda, United States, Ethiopia, and China, listed according to the size of their contribution to population growth. China would be higher still in this list were it not for its 'one child' policy.
- Global life expectancy at birth, which is estimated to have risen from 46 years in 1950-1955 to 65 years in 2000-2005, is expected to keep rising to reach 75 years in 2045-2050. In the more developed regions, the projected increase is from 75 years today to 82 years by mid-century. Among the least developed countries, where life expectancy today is just under 50 years, it is expected to be 66 years in 2045-2050.
- The population of 51 countries or areas, including Germany, Italy, Japan and most of the successor States of the former Soviet Union, is expected to be lower in 2050 than in 2005.
- During 2005-2050, the net number of international migrants to more developed regions is projected to be 98 million. Because deaths are projected to exceed births in the more developed regions by 73 million during 2005-2050, population growth in those regions will largely be due to international migration.
- In 2000-2005, net migration in 28 countries either prevented population decline or doubled at least the contribution of natural increase (births minus deaths) to population growth. These countries include Austria, Canada, Croatia, Denmark, Germany, Italy, Portugal, Qatar, Singapore, Spain, Sweden, United Arab Emirates and United Kingdom.
- Birth rates are now falling in a small percentage of developing countries, while the actual populations in many developed countries would fall without immigration.
- By 2050 (Medium variant), India will have 1.6 billion people, China 1.4 billion, United States 439 million, Pakistan 309 million, Indonesia 280 million, Nigeria 259 million, Bangladesh 258 million, Brazil 245 million, Democratic Republic of the Congo 189 million, Ethiopia 185 million, Philippines 141 million, Mexico 132 million, Egypt 125 million, Vietnam 120 million, Russia 109 million, Japan 103 million, Iran 100 million, Turkey 99 million, Uganda 93 million, Tanzania 85 million, Kenya 85 million and United Kingdom 80 million.

2050

- Africa — 1.9 billion
- Asia — 5.2 billion
- Europe — 674 million
- Latin America & Caribbean — 765 million
- North America — 448 million

The theory of demographic transition held that, after the standard of living and life expectancy increase, family sizes and birth rates decline. However, as new data has become available, it has been observed that after a certain level of development the fertility increases again. This means that both the worry the theory generated about aging populations and the complacency it bred regarding the future environmental impact of population growth are misguided.

Factors cited in the old theory included such social factors as later ages of marriage, the growing desire of many women in such settings to seek careers outside child rearing and domestic work, and the decreased need of children in industrialized settings. The latter factor stems from the fact that children perform a great deal of work in small-scale agricultural societies, and work less in industrial ones; it has been cited to explain the decline in birth rates in industrializing regions.

Another version of demographic transition is proposed by anthropologist Virginia Abernethy in her book *'Population Politics'*, where she claims that the demographic transition occurs primarily in nations where women enjoy a special status. In strongly patriarchal nations, where she claims women enjoy few special rights, a high standard of living tends to result in population growth.

Many countries have high population growth rates but lower total fertility rates because high population growth in the past skewed the age demographic toward a young age, so the population still rises as the more numerous younger generation approaches maturity.

"Demographic entrapment" is a concept developed by Maurice King, Honorary Research Fellow at the University of Leeds, who posits that this phenomenon occurs when a country has a population larger than its carrying capacity, no possibility of migration, and exports too little to be able to import food. This will cause starvation. He claims that for example many sub-Saharan nations are or will become stuck in demographic entrapment, instead of having a demographic transition.

There is wide variability both in the definition and in the proposed size of the Earth's carrying capacity, with estimates ranging from less than 1 to 1000 billion (1 trillion). Around two-thirds of the estimates fall in the range of 4 billion to 16 billion (with unspecified standard errors), with a median of about 10 billion.

In a study titled *'Food, Land, Population and the U.S. Economy'*, David Pimentel, professor of ecology and agriculture at Cornell University, and Mario Giampietro, senior researcher at the US National Research Institute on Food and Nutrition (INRAN), estimate the maximum U.S. population for a sustainable economy at 200 million. According to this theory, in order to achieve a sustainable economy and avert disaster, the United States would have to reduce its population by at least one-third, and world population would have to be reduced by two-thirds.

Some groups (for example, the World Wide Fund for Nature and Global Footprint Network) have stated that the carrying capacity for the human population has been exceeded as measured using the Ecological Footprint. In 2006, WWF's 'Living Planet Report' stated that in order for all humans to live with the current consumption patterns of Europeans, we would be spending three times more than what the planet can renew. Humanity as a whole was using, by 2006, 40 per cent more than what Earth can regenerate.

But critics question the simplifications and statistical methods used in calculating Ecological Footprints. Therefore Global Footprint Network and its partner organizations have engaged with national governments and international agencies to test the results — reviews have been produced by France, Germany, the European Commission, Switzerland, Luxembourg, Japan and the United Arab Emirates. Some point out that a more refined method of assessing Ecological Footprint is to designate sustainable *vs.* non-sustainable categories of consumption. However, if yield estimates were adjusted for sustainable levels of production, the yield figures would be lower, and hence the overshoot estimated by the Ecological Footprint method even higher.

David Pimentel, Professor Emeritus at Cornell University, has stated that "With the imbalance growing between population numbers and vital life sustaining resources, humans must actively conserve cropland, freshwater, energy, and biological resources. There is a need to develop renewable energy resources. Humans everywhere must understand that rapid population growth damages the Earth's resources and diminishes human well-being".

These reflect the comments also of the United States Geological Survey in their paper The Future of Planet Earth: Scientific Challenges in the Coming Century. "As the global population continues to grow...people will place greater and greater demands on the resources of our planet, including mineral and energy resources, open space, water, and plant and animal resources." 'Earth's natural wealth: an audit' by *New Scientist* magazine states that many of the minerals that we use for a variety of products are in danger of running out in the near future . A handful of geologists around the world have calculated the costs of new technologies in terms of the materials they use and the implications of their spreading to the developing world. All agree that the planet's booming population and rising standards of living are set to put unprecedented demands on the materials that only Earth itself can provide. Limitations on how much of these materials is available could even mean that some technologies are not worth pursuing long term. . . . "Virgin stocks of several metals appear inadequate to sustain the modern 'developed world' quality of life for all of Earth's people under contemporary technology."

On the other hand, some researchers, such as Julian Simon and Bjorn Lomborg believe that resources exist for further population growth. However, critics warn, this will be at a high cost to the Earth: "the technological optimists are probably correct in claiming that overall world food production can be increased substantially over the next few decades . . . [however] the environmental cost of what Paul R. and Anne H. Ehrlich describe as 'turning the Earth into a giant human feedlot' could be severe. A large expansion of agriculture to provide growing populations with improved diets is likely to lead to further deforestation, loss of species, soil erosion, and pollution from pesticides and fertilizer runoff as farming intensifies and new land is brought into production." Since we are intimately dependent upon the living systems of the Earth, some scientists have questioned the wisdom of further expansion.

According to the Millennium Ecosystem Assessment, a four-year research effort by 1,360 of the world's leading scientists commissioned to measure the actual value of natural resources to humans and the world, "The structure of the world's ecosystems changed more rapidly in the second half of the twentieth century than at any time in recorded human history, and virtually all of Earth's ecosystems have now been significantly transformed through human actions." "Ecosystem services, particularly food production, timber and fisheries, are important for employment and economic activity. Intensive use of ecosystems often produces the greatest short-term advantage, but excessive and unsustainable use can lead to losses in the long term. A country could cut its forests and deplete its fisheries, and this would show only as a positive gain to GDP, despite the loss of capital assets. If the full economic value of ecosystems were taken into account in decision-making, their degradation could be significantly slowed down or even reversed".

Another study by the United Nations Environment Programme (UNEP) called the Global Environment Outlook which involved 1,400 scientists and took five years to prepare comes to similar conclusions. It "found that human consumption had far outstripped available resources. Each person on Earth now requires a third more land to supply his or her needs than the planet can supply." It faults a failure to "respond to or recognise the magnitude of the challenges facing the people and the environment of the planet . . . 'The systematic destruction of the Earth's natural and nature-based resources has reached a point where the economic viability of economies is being challenged — and where the bill we hand to our children may prove impossible to pay'. . . The report's authors say its objective is 'not to present a dark and gloomy scenario, but an urgent call to action'. It warns that tackling the problems may affect the vested interests of powerful groups, and that the environment must be moved to the core of decision-making.

Although all resources, whether mineral or other, are limited on the planet, there is a degree of self-correction whenever a scarcity or high-demand for a particular kind is experienced. For example in 1990 known reserves of many natural resources were higher, and their prices lower, than in 1970, despite higher demand and higher consumption. Whenever a price spike would occur, the market tended to correct itself whether by substituting an equivalent resource or switching to a new technology.

Fresh Water

Fresh water supplies, on which agriculture depends, are running low worldwide. This water crisis is only expected to worsen as the population increases. Lester R. Brown of the Earth Policy Institute argues that declining water supplies will have future disastrous consequences for agriculture.

Potential problems with dependence on desalination are reviewed below, however, the majority of the world's freshwater supply is contained in the polar icecaps, and underground river systems accessible through springs and wells.

Fresh water can be obtained from salt water by desalination. For example, Malta derives two thirds of its freshwater by desalination. A number of nuclear powered desalination plants exist; these could continuously provide drinking water with few limitations, if the development of breeder reactors results in nuclear fuel becoming a renewable resource. However, the high costs of desalination, especially for poor countries, make impractical the transport of large amounts of desalinated seawater to interiors of large countries. The cost of desalinization varies; Israel is now desalinating water for a cost of 53 cents per cubic metre, Singapore at 49 cents per cubic metre. In the United States, the cost is 81 cents per cubic metre ($3.06 for 1,000 gallons).

According to a 2004 study by Zhoua and Tolb, "one needs to lift the water by 2000 m, or transport it over more than 1600-km to get transport costs equal to the desalination costs. Desalinated water is expensive in places that are both somewhat far from the sea and somewhat high, such as Riyadh and Harare. In other places, the dominant cost is desalination, not transport. This leads to somewhat lower costs in places like Beijing, Bangkok, Zaragoza, Phoenix, and, of course, coastal cities like Tripoli." Thus while the study is generally positive about the technology for affluent areas that are proximate to oceans, it concludes that "Desalinated water may be a solution for some water-stress regions, but not for places that are poor, deep in the interior of a continent, or at high elevation. Unfortunately, that includes some of the places with biggest water problems." Another potential problem with desalination is the byproduction of saline brine, which can be a major cause of marine pollution when dumped back into the oceans at high temperatures."

The world's largest desalination plant is the Jebel Ali Desalination Plant (Phase 2) in the United Arab Emirates, which can produce 300 million cubic meters of water per year, or about 2500 gallons per second. The largest desalination plant in the US is the one at Tampa Bay, Florida, which began desalinizing 25 million gallons (95000 m^3) of water per day in December 2007. A January 17, 2008, article in the *Wall Street Journal* states, "Worldwide, 13,080 desalination plants produce more than 12 billion gallons of water a day, according to the International Desalination Association." After being desalinized at Jubail, Saudi Arabia, water is pumped 200 miles (320-km) inland though a pipeline to the capital city of Riyadh.

Food

Studies agree that there is enough food to support the world population, but critics dispute this, particularly if sustainability is taken into account.

More than 100 countries now import wheat and 40 countries import rice. Egypt and Iran rely on imports for 40 per cent of their grain supply. Algeria, Japan, South Korea and Taiwan import 70 per cent or more. Yemen and Israel import more than 90 per cent. And just 6 countries — Argentina, Australia, Canada, France, Thailand and the USA — supply 90 per cent of grain exports. In recent decades the US alone supplied almost half of world grain exports.

A 2001 United Nations report says population growth is 'the main force driving increases in agricultural demand' but "most recent expert assessments are cautiously optimistic about the ability of global food production to keep up with demand for the foreseeable future (that is to say, until approximately 2030 or 2050)", assuming declining population growth rates.

However, the observed figures for 2007 show an actual increase in absolute numbers of undernourished people in the world, 923 million in 2007 *vs.* 832 million in 1995.; the more recent FAO estimates point out to an even more dramatic increase, to 1.02 billion in 2009.

The amounts of natural resources in this context are not necessarily fixed, and their distribution is not necessarily a zero-sum game. For example, due to the Green Revolution and the fact that more and more land is appropriated each year from wild lands for agricultural purposes, the worldwide production of food had steadily increased up until 1995. World food production per person was considerably higher in 2005 than 1961.

As world population doubled from 3 billion to 6 billion, daily Calorie consumption in poor countries increased from 1,932 to 2,650, and the percentage of people in those countries who were malnourished fell from 45 per cent to 18 per cent. This suggests that Third World poverty and famine are caused by underdevelopment, not overpopulation. However, others question these statistics. From 1950 to 1984, as the Green Revolution transformed agriculture around the world, grain production increased by over 250 per cent. The world population has grown by about four billion since the beginning of the Green Revolution and most believe that, without the Revolution, there would be greater famine and malnutrition than the UN presently documents.

The number of people who are overweight has surpassed the number who are undernourished. In a 2006 news story, MSNBC reported, "There are an estimated 800 million undernourished people and more than a billion considered overweight worldwide." The U.S. has one of the highest rates of obesity in the world.

The Food and Agriculture Organization of the United Nations states in its report *'The State of Food Insecurity in the World 2006'*, that while the number of undernourished people in the developing countries has declined by about three million, a smaller proportion of the populations of developing countries is undernourished today than in 1990–92: 17 per cent against 20 per cent. Furthermore, FAO's projections suggest that the proportion of hungry people in developing countries could be halved from 1990-92 levels to 10 per cent by 2015. The FAO also states "We have emphasized first and foremost that reducing hunger is no longer a question of means in the hands of the global community. The world is richer today than it was ten years ago. There is more food available and still more could be produced without excessive upward pressure on prices. The knowledge and resources to reduce hunger are there. What is lacking is sufficient political will to mobilize those resources to the benefit of the hungry".

As of 2008, the price of grain has increased due to more farming used in biofuels, world oil prices at over $100 a barrel, global population growth, climate change, loss of agricultural land to residential and industrial development, and growing consumer demand in China and India Food riots have recently taken place in many countries across the world. An epidemic of stem rust on wheat caused by race Ug99 is currently spreading across Africa and into Asia and is causing major concern. A virulent wheat disease could destroy most of the world's main wheat crops, leaving millions to starve. The fungus has spread from Africa to Iran, and may already be in Afghanistan and Pakistan.

It is becoming increasingly difficult to maintain food security in a world beset by a confluence of 'peak' phenomena, namely peak oil, peak water, peak phosphorus, peak grain and peak fish. Growing populations, falling energy sources and food shortages will create the 'perfect storm' by 2030, according to the UK government chief scientist. He said food reserves are at a 50-year low but the world requires 50 per cent more energy, food and water by 2030. The world will have to produce 70 per cent more food by 2050 to feed a projected extra 2.3 billion people, the United Nations' Food and Agriculture Organisation (FAO) warned.

Population as a Function of Food Availability

Thinkers such as David Pimentel, a professor from Cornell University, Virginia Abernethy, Alan Thornhill, Russell Hopffenberg and author Daniel Quinn propose that like all other animals, human populations predictably grow and shrink according to their available food supply — populations grow in an abundance of food, and shrink in times of scarcity.

Proponents of this theory argue that every time food production is increased, the population grows. Some human populations throughout history support this theory. Populations of hunter-gatherers fluctuate in accordance with the amount of available food. Population increased after the Neolithic Revolution and an increased food supply. This was followed by subsequent population growth after subsequent agricultural revolutions.

Critics of this idea point out that birth rates are lowest in the developed nations, which also have the highest access to food. In fact, some developed countries have both a diminishing population and an abundant food supply. The United Nations projects that the population of 51 countries or areas, including Germany, Italy, Japan and most of the states of the former Soviet Union, is expected to be lower in 2050 than in 2005. This shows that when one limits their scope to the population living within a given political boundary, human populations do not always grow to match the available food supply. Additionally, many of these countries are major *exporters* of food.

Nevertheless, on the global scale the world population is increasing, as is the net quantity of human food produced - a pattern that has been true for roughly 10,000 years, since the human development of agriculture. That some countries demonstrate negative population growth fails to discredit the theory. Food moves across borders from areas of abundance to areas of scarcity. Additionally, this hypothesis is not so simplistic as to be rejected by a single case study, as in Germany's recent population trends — clearly other factors are at work: contraceptive access, cultural norms and most importantly economic realities differ from nation to nation.

As a Result of Water Deficits

Water deficits, which are already spurring heavy grain imports in numerous smaller countries, may soon do the same in larger countries, such as China or India, if technology is not used. The water tables are falling in scores of countries (including Northern China, the US, and India) owing to widespread overdrafting beyond sustainable yields. Other countries affected include Pakistan, Iran, and Mexico. This overdrafting is already leading to water scarcity and cutbacks in grain harvest. Even with the overpumping of its aquifers, China has developed a grain deficit. This effect has contributed in driving grain prices upward. Most of the 3 billion people projected to be added worldwide by mid-century will be born in countries already experiencing water shortages. One suggested solution is for population growth to be slowed quickly by investing heavily in female literacy and family planning services. Desalination is also considered a viable and effective solution to the problem of water shortages.

After China and India, there is a second tier of smaller countries with large water deficits — Algeria, Egypt, Iran, Mexico, and Pakistan. Four of these already import a large share of their grain. Only Pakistan remains self-sufficient. But with a population expanding by 4 million a year, it will also soon turn to the world market for grain.

Land

The World Resources Institute states that "Agricultural conversion to croplands and managed pastures has affected some 3.3 billion [hectares] — roughly 26 per cent of the land area. All totalled, agriculture has displaced one-third of temperate and tropical forests and one-quarter of natural grasslands." Forty per cent of the land area is under conversion and fragmented; less than one quarter, primarily in the Arctic and the deserts, remains intact. Usable land may become less useful through salinization, deforestation, desertification, erosion, and urban sprawl. Global warming may cause flooding of many of the most productive agricultural areas. The development of energy sources may also require large areas, for example, the building of hydroelectric dams. Thus, available useful land may become a limiting factor. By most estimates, at least half of cultivable land is already being farmed, and there are concerns that the remaining reserves are greatly overestimated.

High crop yield vegetables like potatoes and lettuce use less space on inedible plant parts, like stalks, husks, vines, and inedible leaves. New varieties of selectively bred and hybrid plants have larger edible parts (fruit, vegetable, grain) and smaller inedible parts; however, many of the gains of agricultural technology are now historic, and new advances are more difficult to achieve. With new technologies, it is possible to grow crops on some marginal land under certain conditions. Aquaculture could theoretically increase available area. Hydroponics and food from bacteria and fungi, like quorn, may allow the growing of food without having to consider land quality, climate, or even available sunlight, although such a process may be very energy-intensive. Some argue that not all arable land will remain productive if used for agriculture because some marginal land can only be made to produce food by unsustainable practices like slash-and-burn agriculture. Even with the modern techniques of agriculture, the sustainability of production is in question.

Some countries, such as the United Arab Emirates and particularly the Emirate of Dubai have constructed large artificial islands, or have created large dam and dike systems, like the Netherlands, which reclaim land from the sea to increase their total land area. Some scientists have said that in the future, densely populated cities will use vertical farming to grow food inside skyscrapers. The notion that space is limited has been decried by skeptics, who point out that the Earth's population of roughly 6.8 billion people could comfortably inhabit an area comparable in size to the state of Texas, in the United States (about 269,000 square miles or 696,707 km^2). However, the impact of humanity extends over a far greater area than that required simply for habitation.

Fossil Fuels

Population optimists have been criticized for failing to take into account the depletion of the petroleum required for the production of fertilizers and fuel for transportation, as well as other fossil fuels. In his 1992 book *'Earth in the Balance*, Al Gore wrote', ". . . it ought to be possible to establish a coordinated global programme to accomplish the strategic goal of completely eliminating the internal combustion engine over, say, a twenty-five-year period. . ." Approximately half of the oil produced in the United States is refined into gasoline for use in internal combustion engines.

Optimists counter that fossil fuels will be sufficient until the development and implementation of suitable replacement technologies–such as hydrogen or other sources of renewable energy—occurs. Methods of manufacturing fertilizers from garbage, sewage, and agricultural waste by using thermal depolymerization have been discovered.

Overpopulation has substantially adversely impacted the environment of Earth starting at least as early as the 20th century. There are also economic consequences of this environmental degradation in the form of ecosystem services attrition. Beyond the scientifically verifiable harm to the environment, some assert the moral right of other species to simply exist rather than become extinct. Environmental author Jeremy Rifkin has said that "our burgeoning population and urban way of life have been purchased at the expense of vast ecosystems and habitats. . . . It's no accident that as we celebrate the urbanization of the world, we are quickly approaching another historic watershed: the disappearance of the wild".

Says Peter Raven, former President of the American Association for the Advancement of Science (AAAS) in their seminal work AAAS Atlas of Population and Environment, "Where do we stand in our efforts to achieve a sustainable world? Clearly, the past half century has been a traumatic one, as the collective impact of human numbers, affluence (consumption per individual) and our choices of technology continue to exploit rapidly an increasing proportion of the world's resources at an unsustainable rate. . . . During a remarkably short period of time, we have lost a quarter of the world's topsoil and a fifth of its agricultural land, altered the composition of the atmosphere profoundly, and destroyed a major proportion of our forests and other natural habitats without replacing them. Worst of all, we have driven the rate of biological extinction, the permanent loss of species, up several hundred times beyond its historical levels, and are threatened with the loss of a majority of all species by the end of the 21st century".

Further, even in countries which have both large population growth and major ecological problems, it is not necessarily true that curbing the population growth will make a major contribution towards resolving all environmental problems. However, as developing countries with high populations become more industrialized, pollution and consumption will invariably increase.

The Worldwatch Institute said the booming economies of China and India are planetary powers that are shaping the global biosphere. The report states:

"The world's ecological capacity is simply insufficient to satisfy the ambitions of China, India, Japan, Europe and the United States as well as the aspirations of the rest of the world in a sustainable way".

It said that if China and India were to consume as much resources per capita as United States or Japan in 2030 together they would require a full planet Earth to meet their needs. In the longterm these effects can lead to increased conflict over dwindling resources and in the worst case a Malthusian catastrophe. Many studies link population growth with emissions and the effect of climate change.

In 1800 only 3 per cent of the world's population lived in cities. By the 20th century's close, 47 per cent did so. In 1950, there were 83 cities with populations exceeding one million; but by 2007, this had risen to 468 agglomerations of more than one million. If the trend continues, the world's urban population will double every 38 years, say researchers. The UN forecasts that today's urban population of 3.2 billion will rise to nearly 5 billion by 2030, when three out of five people will live in cities.

The increase will be most dramatic in the poorest and least-urbanised continents, Asia and Africa. Projections indicate that most urban growth over the next 25 years will be in developing countries. One billion people, one-sixth of the world's population, or one-third of urban population, now live in shanty towns, which are seen as 'breeding grounds' for social problems such as crime, drug addiction, alcoholism, poverty and unemployment. In many poor countries, slums exhibit high rates of disease due to unsanitary conditions, malnutrition, and lack of basic health care.

In 2000, there were 18 megacities — conurbations such as Tokyo, Seoul, Mexico City, Mumbai, São Paulo and New York City — that have populations in excess of 10 million inhabitants. Greater Tokyo already has 35 million, more than the entire population of Canada (at 34.1 million).

By 2025, according to the *Far Eastern Economic Review*, Asia alone will have at least 10 hypercities, those with 20 million or more, including Jakarta (24.9 million people), Dhaka (25 million), Karachi (26.5 million), Shanghai (27 million) and Mumbai (33 million). Lagos has grown from 300,000 in 1950 to an estimated 15 million today, and the Nigerian government estimates that city will have expanded to 25 million residents by 2015. Chinese experts forecast that Chinese cities will contain 800 million people by 2020.

Despite the increase in population density within cities (and the emergence of megacities), UN Habitat states in its reports that urbanization may be the best compromise in the face of global population growth. Cities concentrate human activity within limited areas, limiting the breadth of environmental damage. But this mitigating influence can only be achieved if urban planning is significantly improved and city services are properly maintained.

Ecological Footprint by World Region

As set forth on page 18 of WWF's Living Planet report, the regions of the world with the greatest ecological footprint are ranked as follows as of 2003:

- North America
- Europe (European Union countries)
- Middle-East and Central Asia
- Asia and Pacific Islands
- Africa
- Europe (Non-European Union countries)
- Latin-America and the Caribbean
- Australia and New Zealand

Effects of Human Overpopulation

Some problems associated with or exacerbated by human overpopulation:

- Inadequate fresh water for drinking water use as well as sewage treatment and effluent discharge. Some countries, like Saudi Arabia, use energy-expensive desalination to solve the problem of water shortages.
- Depletion of natural resources, especially fossil fuels.
- Increased levels of air pollution, water pollution, soil contamination and noise pollution. Once a country has industrialized and become wealthy, a combination of government regulation and technological innovation causes pollution to decline substantially, even as the population continues to grow.
- Deforestation and loss of ecosystems that sustain global atmospheric oxygen and carbon dioxide balance; about eight million hectares of forest are lost each year.
- Changes in atmospheric composition and consequent global warming.
- Irreversible loss of arable land and increases in desertification Deforestation and desertification can be reversed by adopting property rights, and this policy is successful even while the human population continues to grow.
- Mass species extinctions. from reduced habitat in tropical forests due to slash-and-burn techniques that sometimes are practiced by hifting

cultivators, especially in countries with rapidly expanding rural populations; present extinction rates may be as high as 140,000 species lost per year. As of 2008, the IUCN Red List lists a total of 717 animal species having gone extinct during recorded human history.

- High infant and child mortality High rates of infant mortality are caused by poverty. Rich countries with high population densities have low rates of infant mortality.
- Intensive factory farming to support large populations. It results in human threats including the evolution and spread of antibiotic resistant bacteria diseases, excessive air and water pollution, and new virus that infect humans.
- Increased chance of the emergence of new epidemics and pandemics For many environmental and social reasons, including overcrowded living conditions, malnutrition and inadequate, inaccessible, or non-existent health care, the poor are more likely to be exposed to infectious diseases.
- Starvation, malnutrition or poor diet with ill health and diet-deficiency diseases (e.g. rickets). However, rich countries with high population densities do not have famine.
- Poverty coupled with inflation in some regions and a resulting low level of capital formation. Poverty and inflation are aggravated by bad government and bad economic policies. Many countries with high population densities have eliminated absolute poverty and keep their inflation rates very low.
- Low life expectancy in countries with fastest growing populations.
- Unhygienic living conditions for many based upon water resource depletion, discharge of raw sewage and solid waste disposal. However, this problem can be reduced with the adoption of sewers. For example, after Karachi, Pakistan installed sewers, its infant mortality rate fell substantially.
- Elevated crime rate due to drug cartels and increased theft by people stealing resources to survive.
- Conflict over scarce resources and crowding, leading to increased levels of warfare.
- Less Personal Freedom/More Restrictive Laws. Laws regulate interactions between humans. Law "serves as a primary social mediator of relations between people". The higher the population density, the more frequent such interactions become, and thus there develops a need for more laws and/or more restrictive laws to regulate these interactions.

It is even speculated that democracy is threatened due to overpopulation, and could give rise to totalitarian style governments.

Some economists, such as Thomas Sowell and Walter E. Williams argue that third world poverty and famine are caused in part by bad government and bad economic policies. Most biologists and sociologists see overpopulation as a serious threat to the quality of human life.

Overpopulation and Warfare

The hypothesis that population pressure causes increased warfare has been recently criticized on the empirical grounds. Both studies focussing on specific historical societies and analyses of cross-cultural data have failed to find positive correlation between population density and incidence of warfare. Andrey Korotayev, in collaboration with Peter Turchin, has shown that such negative results do not falsify the population-warfare hypothesis. Population and warfare are dynamical variables, and if their interaction causes sustained oscillations, then we do not in general expect to find strong correlation between the two variables measured at the same time (that is, unlagged). Korotayev and Turchin have explored mathematically what the dynamical patterns of interaction between population and warfare (focusing on internal warfare) might be in both stateless and state societies. Next, they have tested the model predictions in several empirical case studies: early modern England, Han and Tang China, and the Roman Empire. Their empirical results have supported the population-warfare theory: Korotayev and Turchin have found that there is a tendency for population numbers and internal warfare intensity to oscillate with the same period but shifted in phase (with warfare peaks following population peaks). Furthermore, they have demonstrated that in the agrarian societies the rates of change of the two variables behave precisely as predicted by the theory: population rate of change is negatively affected by warfare intensity, while warfare rate of change is positively affected by population density.

Mitigation Measures

While the current world trends are not indicative of any realistic solution to human overpopulation during the 21st century, there are several mitigation measures that have or can be applied to reduce the adverse impacts of overpopulation.

Birth Regulations

Overpopulation is related to the issue of birth control; some nations, like the People's Republic of China, use strict measures to reduce birth rates. Religious and ideological opposition to birth control has been cited as a factor contributing to overpopulation and poverty. Some leaders and environmentalists (such as Ted Turner) have suggested that there is an urgent need to strictly implement a China-like one-child policy globally by the United Nations, because this would help control and reduce population gradually.

Indira Gandhi, late Prime Minister of India, implemented a forced sterilization programme in the 1970s. Officially, men with two children or more had to submit to sterilization, but many unmarried young men, political opponents and ignorant men were also believed to have been sterilized. This programme is still remembered and criticized in India, and is blamed for creating a public aversion to family planning, which hampered Government programmes for decades.

Urban designer Michael E. Arth has proposed a "choice-based, marketable birth license plan" he calls "birth credits." Birth credits would allow any woman to have as many children as she wants, as long as she buys a license for any children beyond an average allotment that would result in zero population growth (ZPG). If that allotment was determined to be one child, for example, then the first child would be free, and the market would determine what the licence fee for each additional child would cost. Extra credits would expire after a certain time, so these credits could not be hoarded by speculators. Another advantage of the scheme is that the affluent would not buy them because they already limit their family size by choice, as evidenced by an average of 1.1 children per European woman. The actual cost of the credits would only be a fraction of the actual cost of having and raising a child, so the credits would serve more as a wake-up call to women who might otherwise produce children without seriously considering the long term consequences to themselves or society.

Education and Empowerment

One option is to focus on education about overpopulation, family planning, and birth control methods, and to make birth-control devices like male/female condoms, pills and intrauterine devices easily available. Some 80 million pregnancies — nearly 40 per cent of the total each year – are unplanned. An estimated 350 million women in the poorest countries of the world either did not want their last child, do not want another child or want to space their pregnancies, but they lack access to information, affordable means and services to determine the size and spacing of their families. In the developing world, some 514,000 women die annually of complications from pregnancy and abortion. Slightly more than one half of the maternal deaths occurred in the sub-Saharan Africa region, followed by South Asia. Additionally, 8 million infants die, many because of malnutrition or preventable diseases, especially from lack of access to clean drinking water. In the United States, in 2001, almost half of pregnancies were unintended.

Egypt announced a programme to reduce its overpopulation by family planning education and putting women in the workforce. It was announced in June 2008 by the Minister of Health and Population Hatem el-Gabali. The government has set aside 480 million Egyptian pounds (about 90 million U.S. dollars) for the programme.

In the 1970s, Gerard O'Neill suggested building space habitats that could support 30,000 times the carrying capacity of Earth using just the asteroid belt and that the solar system as a whole could sustain current population growth rates for a thousand years. Marshall Savage has projected a human population of five quintillion throughout the solar system by 3000, with the majority in the asteroid belt. Arthur C. Clarke prophesied there could be humans on the Moon, Mars, Europa, Ganymede, Titan and in orbit around Venus, Neptune and Pluto in 2057. Freeman Dyson favours the Kuiper belt as the future home of humanity, suggesting this could happen within a few centuries. In *Mining the Sky*, John S. Lewis suggests that the resources of the solar system could support 10 quadrillion (10^{16}) people.

K. Eric Drexler, famous inventor of the futuristic concept of molecular nanotechnology, has suggested in *Engines of Creation* that colonizing space will mean breaking the Malthusian limits to growth for the human species.

CHAPTER 7

Overexploitation

Overexploitation, also called overharvesting, refers to harvesting a renewable resource to the point of diminishing returns. If sustained, it can lead to the destruction of the resource. The term can be applied to various natural resources such as wild medicinal plants, grazing pastures, fish stocks, forests and water aquifers.

In ecology, overexploitation describes one of the five main activities threatening global biodiversity. Ecologists use the term to describe populations that are harvested at a rate that is unsustainable, given their natural rates of mortality and capacities for reproduction. This can result in extinction at the population level and even extinction of whole species. In conservation biology the term is usually used in the context of human economic activity that involves the taking of biological resources, or organisms, in larger numbers than their populations can withstand. The term is also used and defined somewhat differently in fisheries, hydrology and natural resource management.

Overexploitation can lead to resource destruction, including extinctions. However it is also possible for overexploitation to be sustainable, as discussed below in the section on fisheries. In the context of fishing, the term overfishing can be used instead of overexploitation, as can overgrazing in stock management, overlogging in forest management, overdrafting in aquifer management, and endangered species in species monitoring. Overexploitation is not an activity limited to humans. Introduced predators and herbivores, for example, can overexploit native flora and fauna.

Overexploitation is not a new phenomenon. It has been observed for millennia. For example, ceremonial cloaks worn by the Hawaiian kings were made from the mamo bird; a single cloak used the feathers of 70,000 birds of this now-extinct species. The dodo, a flightless bird from Mauritius, is another well known example of overexploitation. As with many island species, it was naive about certain predators, allowing humans to approach and kill it with ease.

From the earliest of times, hunting for wild mammals and birds has been an important human activity as a means of survival. There is a whole history of overexploitation in the form of overhunting. The overkill hypothesis (Quaternary extinction events) explains why the megafaunal extinctions occurred within a relatively short period of time. This can be traced with human migration. The most convincing evidence of this theory is that 80 per cent of the North American large mammal species disappeared within 1000 years of the arrival of humans on the western hemisphere continents. Again, in New Zealand, ten species of the giant moa birds were hunted to extinction by the Maori by 1500 AD. A second wave of extinctions occurred later with European settlement.

In more recent times, overexploitation has resulted in the gradual emergence of the concepts of sustainability and sustainable development, which has built on other concepts, such as sustainable yield, eco-development and deep ecology.

Overexploitation need not necessarily lead to the destruction of the resource, nor is it necessarily unsustainable. However, depleting the numbers or amount of the resource can change its quality. For example, footstool palm is a wild palm tree found in Southeast Asia. Its leaves are used for thatching and food wrapping, and overharvesting has resulted in its leaf size becoming smaller.

Tragedy of the Commons

The tragedy of the commons refers to a dilemma described in an article by that name written by Garrett Hardin and first published in the journal *Science* in 1968.

Central to Hardin's essay is an example which is a useful parable for understanding how overexploitation can occur.

This example was first sketched in an 1833 pamphlet by William Forster Lloyd, as a hypothetical and simplified situation based on mediaeval land tenure in Europe, of herders sharing a commons on which they are each entitled to let their cows graze. In Hardin's example, it is in each herder's interest to put each succeeding cow he acquires onto the land, even if the carrying capacity of the common is exceeded and it is temporarily or permanently damaged for all as a result. The herder receives all of the benefits from an additional cow, while the damage to the common is shared by the entire group. If all herders make this individually rational economic decision, the common will be overexploited or even destroyed to the detriment of all.

However, since all herders reach the same rational conclusion, overexploitation in the form of overgrazing occurs, with immediate losses, and the pasture may be degraded to the point where it gives very little return.

"Therein is the tragedy. Each man is locked into a system that compels him to increase his herd without limit — in a world that is limited. Ruin is the destination toward which all men rush, each pursuing his own interest in a society that believes in the freedom of the commons".

In the course of his essay, Hardin develops the theme, drawing in many examples of latter day commons, such as national parks, the atmosphere, oceans, rivers and fish stocks. The example of fish stocks had led some to call this the 'tragedy of the fishers'. A major theme running through the essay is the growth of human populations, with the Earth's finite resources being the general common.

The tragedy of the commons has intellectual roots tracing back to Aristotle, who noted that "what is common to the greatest number has the least care bestowed upon it", as well as to Hobbes and his leviathan. The opposite situation to a tragedy of the commons is sometimes referred to as a tragedy of the anticommons: a situation in which rational individuals, acting separately, collectively waste a given resource by underutilizing it.

The tragedy of the commons can be avoided if it is appropriately regulated. Hardin's use of 'commons' has frequently been misunderstood, leading Hardin to later remark that he should have titled his work 'The tragedy of the unregulated commons'.

Fisheries

In wild fisheries, overexploitation or overfishing occurs when a fish stock has been fished down "below the size that, on average, would support the long-term maximum sustainable yield of the fishery". However, overexploitation can be sustainable.

When a fishery starts harvesting fish from a previously unexploited stock, the biomass of the fish stock will decrease, since harvesting means fish are being removed. For sustainability, the rate at which the fish replenish biomass through reproduction must balance the rate at which the fish are being harvested. If the harvest rate is increased, then the stock biomass will further decrease. At a certain point, the maximum harvest yield that can be sustained will be reached, and further attempts to increase the harvest rate will result in the collapse of the fishery. This point is called the maximum sustainable yield, and in practice, usually occurs when the fishery has been fished down to about 30 per cent of the biomass it had before harvesting started.

It is possible to fish the stock down further, to say 15 per cent of the pre-harvest biomass, and then adjust the harvest rate so the biomass remains at that level. In this case, the fishery is sustainable, but is now overexploited, because the stock has been run down to the point where the sustainable yield is less than it could be.

Fish stocks are said to 'collapse' if their biomass declines by more than 95 percent of their maximum historical biomass. Atlantic cod stocks were severely overexploited in the 1970s and 1980s, leading to their abrupt collapse in 1992. Even though fishing has ceased, the cod stocks have failed to recover. The absence of cod as the apex predator in many areas has led to trophic cascades.

About 25 per cent of world fisheries are now overexploited to the point where their current biomass is less than the level that maximizes their sustainable yield. These depleted fisheries can often recover if fishing pressure is reduced until the stock biomass returns to the optimal biomass. At this point, harvesting can be resumed near the maximum sustainable yield.

The tragedy of the commons can be avoided within the context of fisheries if fishing effort and practices are regulated appropriately by fisheries management. One effective approach may be assigning some measure of ownership in the form of individual transferable quotas (ITQs) to fishermen. In 2008, a large scale study of fisheries that used ITQs, and ones that didn't, provided strong evidence that ITQs help prevent collapses and restore fisheries that appear to be in decline.

Water resource, such as lakes and aquifers, are usually renewable resources which naturally recharge (the term fossil water is sometimes used to describe aquifers which don't recharge). Overexploitation occurs if a water resource, such as the Ogallala Aquifer, is mined or extracted at a rate that exceeds the recharge rate, that is, at a rate that exceeds the practical sustained yield. Recharge usually comes from area streams, rivers and lakes. An aquifer which has been overexploited is said to be overdrafted or depleted. Forests enhance the recharge of aquifers in some locales, although generally forests are a major source of aquifer depletion. Depleted aquifers can become polluted with contaminants such as nitrates, or permanently damaged through subsidence or through saline intrusion from the ocean.

This turns much of the world's underground water and lakes into finite resources with peak usage debates similar to oil. These debates usually centre around agriculture and suburban water usage but generation of electricity from nuclear energy or coal and tar sands mining is also water resource intensive. A modified Hubbert curve applies to any resource that can be harvested faster than it can be replaced. Though Hubbert's original analysis did not apply to renewable resources, their overexploitation can result in a Hubbert-like peak. This has led to the concept of peak water.

Forests are overexploited when they are logged at a rate faster than reforestation takes place. Reforestation competes with other land uses such as food production, livestock grazing, and living space for further economic growth. Historically utilization of forest products, including timber and fuel wood, have played a key role in human societies, comparable to the roles of water and cultivable land. Today, developed countries continue to utilize timber for building houses, and wood pulp for paper. In developing countries almost three billion people rely on wood for heating and cooking. Short-term economic gains made by conversion of forest to agriculture, or overexploitation of wood products, typically leads to loss of long-term income and long term biological productivity (hence reduction in nature's services). West Africa, Madagascar, Southeast Asia and many other regions have experienced lower revenue because of overexploitation and the consequent declining timber harvests.

Overexploitation is one of the five main activities threatening global biodiversity. The other four activities are pollution, introduced species, habitat fragmentation and habitat destruction.

One of the key health issues associated with biodiversity is drug discovery and the availability of medicinal resources. A significant proportion of drugs are derived, directly or indirectly, from biological sources. Marine ecosystems are of particular interest in this regard. However unregulated and inappropriate bioprospecting can be considered a form of overexploitation which has the potential to degrade ecosystems and increase biodiversity loss, as well as impacting on the rights of the communities and states from which the resources are taken.

Overexploitation threatens one-third of endangered vertebrates, as well as other groups. Excluding edible fish, the illegal trade in wildlife is valued at $10 billion per year. Industries responsible for this include the trade in bushmeat, the trade in Chinese medicine, and the fur trade. The Convention for International Trade in Endangered Species of Wild Fauna and Flora, or CITES was set up in order to control and regulate the trade in endangered animals. It currently protects, to a varying degree, some 33,000 species of animals and plants. It is estimated that a quarter of the endangered vertebrates in the United States of America and half of the endangered mammals is attributed to overexploitation.

All living organisms require resources to survive. Overexploitation of these resources for protracted periods can deplete natural stocks to the point where they are unable to recover within a short time frame. Humans have always harvested food and other resources they have needed to survive. Human populations, historically, were small, and methods of collection limited to small quantities. With an exponential increase in human population, expanding markets and increasing demand, combined with improved access and techniques for capture, are causing the exploitation of many species beyond sustainable levels. In practical terms, if continued, it reduces valuable resources to such low levels that their exploitation is no longer sustainable and can lead to the extinction of a species, in addition to having dramatic, unforeseen effects, on the ecosystem. Overexploitation often occurs rapidly as markets open, utilising previously untapped resources, or locally used species.

Today, overexploitation and misuse of natural resources is an ever present threat for species richness. This is more prevalent when looking at island ecology and the species that inhabit them, as islands can be viewed as the world in miniature. Island endemic populations are more prone to extinction from overexploitation, as they often exist at low densities with reduced reproductive rates. A good example of this are island snails, such as the Hawaiian *Achatinella* and the French Polynesian *Partula*. Achatinelline snails have 15 species listed as extinct and 24 critically endangered while 60 species of partulidae are considered extinct with 14 listed as critically endangered. The WCMC have attributed over-collecting and very low lifetime fecundity for the extreme vulnerability exhibited among these species.

As another example, when the humble hedgehog was introduced to the Scottish island of Uist, the population greatly expanded and took to consuming and overexploiting shorebird eggs, with drastic consequences for their breeding success. Twelve species of avifauna are affected, with some species numbers being reduced by 39 per cent.

Where there is substantial human migration, civil unrest, or war, controls may no longer exist. With civil unrest, for example in the Congo and Rwanda, firearms have become common place and the breakdown of food distribution networks in such countries leaves the resources of the natural environment vulnerable to whoever can exploit them. Animals are even killed as target practice sometimes, or simply to spite the government. Populations of large primates, such as gorillas and chimpanzees, ungulates and other mammals, may be reduced by 80 per cent or more by hunting and certain species may be eliminated all together. This decline has been called the bushmeat crisis.

Overall, 50 bird species that have become extinct since 1500 (approximately 40% of the total) have been subject to overexploitation, including:

- *Great Auk*— The penguin-like bird of the north, hunted for its feathers, meat, fat and oil.
- *Carolina parakeet*— The only parrot species native to the eastern United States, was hunted for crop protection and its feathers.

Other species affected by overexploitation include:

The international trade in fur: chinchilla, vicuña, giant otter and numerous cat species. *Insect collectors:* butterflies Horticulturists: New Zealand mistletoe (*Trilepidia adamsii*), orchids, cacti and many other plant species. *Shell collectors:* Marine molluscs Aquarium hobbyists: tropical fish Chinese medicine: bears, tigers Novelty pets: snakes, parrots and primates.

Overexploitation of species can result in knock-on or cascade effects. This can particularly apply if, through overexploitation, a habitat loses its apex predator. Because of the loss of the top predator, a dramatic increase in their prey species can occur. In turn, the unchecked prey can then overexploit their own food resources until population numbers dwindle, possibly to the point of extinction.

A classic example of cascade effects occurred with sea otters. Starting before the 17th century and not phased out until 1911, sea otters were hunted aggressively for their exceptionally warm and valuable pelts, which could fetch up to US$ 2500. This caused cascade effects through the kelp forest ecosystems along the Pacific Coast of North America.

One of the sea otters' primary food sources is the sea urchin. When hunters caused sea otter populations to decline, an ecological release of sea urchin populations occurred. The sea urchins then overexploited their main food source, kelp, creating urchin barrens, areas of seabed denuded of kelp, but carpeted with urchins. No longer having food to eat, the sea urchin became locally extinct as well. Also, since kelp forest ecosystems are homes to many other species, the loss of the kelp caused other cascade effects of secondary extinctions.

In 1911, when only one small group of 32 sea otters survived in a remote cove, an international treaty was signed to prevent further exploitation of the sea otters. Under heavy protection, the otters multiplied and repopulated the depleted areas, which slowly recovered. More recently, with declining numbers of fish stocks, again due to overexploitation, killer whales have experienced a food shortage and have been observed feeding on sea otters, again reducing their numbers.

CHAPTER 8

Resilience (Ecology)

In ecology, resilience is one possible ecosystem response to a perturbation or disturbance. A resilient ecosystem resists damage and recovers quickly from stochastic disturbances such as fires, flooding, windstorms, insect population explosions, and human activities such as deforestation and the introduction of exotic plant or animal species. Disturbances of sufficient magnitude or duration can profoundly affect an ecosystem and may force an ecosystem to reach a threshold beyond which a different regime of processes and structures predominates . Human activities that adversely affect ecosystem resilience such as reduction of biodiversity, exploitation of natural resources, pollution, land-use, and anthropogenic climate change and are increasingly causing regime shifts in ecosystems, often to less desirable and degraded conditions. Interdisciplinary discourse on resilience now includes consideration of the interactions of humans and ecosystems via socio-ecological systems, and the need for shift from the maximum sustainable yield paradigm to environmental management which aims to build ecological resilience through "resilience analysis, adaptive resource management, and adaptive governance".

The concept of resilience in ecological systems was first introduced by the Canadian ecologist C.S. Holling in order to describe the persistence of natural systems in the face of changes in ecosystem variables due to natural or anthropogenic causes. Resilience has been defined in two ways in ecological literature:

> As the time required for an ecosystem to return to an equilibrium or steady-state following a perturbation (which is also defined as stability by some authors). This definition of resilience is used in other fields such as physics and engineering, and hence has been termed 'engineering resilience' by Holling.

As "the capacity of a system to absorb disturbance and reorganize while undergoing change so as to still retain essentially the same function, structure, identity, and feedbacks."

The second definition has been termed 'ecological resilience', and it presumes the existence of multiple stable states or domains.

Temperate lakes can exist with clear water providing many ecosystem services, or turbid water with toxic algae blooms and reduced ecosystem services. The regime or state is dependent upon lake phosphorous cycles, and either state can be resilient dependent upon management.

Mulga woodlands of Australia can exist in a grass-rich state that supports sheep herding, or a shrub-dominated state of no value for sheep grazing. Changes in regime or state are driven by the interaction of fire, herbivory, and variable rainfall. Either state can be resilient dependent upon management.

Aspects of resilience and changes in stability landscapes.

Aspects of Resilience

Ecologists Brian Walker, Holling and others describe four critical aspects of resilience: *latitude, resistance, precariousness*, and *panarchy*.

The first three can apply both to a whole system or the sub-systems that make it up.

Latitude: the maximum amount a system can be changed before losing its ability to recover (before crossing a threshold which, if breached, makes recovery difficult or impossible).

Resistance: the ease or difficulty of changing the system; how 'resistant' it is to being changed.

Precariousness: how close the current state of the system is to a limit or 'threshold'.

Panarchy: the degree to which a certain hierarchical level of an ecosystem is influenced by other levels. For example, organisms living in communities that are in isolation from one another may be organized differently than the same type of organism living in a large continuous population, thus the community-level structure is influenced by population-level interactions.

These four dimensions are most easily understood through mathematical representation of an ecosystem and its variables in phase space. A phase or state space diagram is one in which each axis represents a variable of a system with any number of variables, so a point in this space describes the system's total state. A state space diagram of an ecosystem would contain several attractors, or *'basins of attraction'* which are representations of ecosystem process configurations or regimes. Moreover, these configurations or regimes can change over time as a result of both internal and external processes.

Closely linked to resilience is *adaptive capacity*, which is the property of an ecosystem that describes change in stability landscapes and resilience. Adaptive capacity in socio-ecological systems refers to the ability of humans to deal with change in their environment by observation, learning and altering their interactions.

Human Impacts on Resilience

Resilience refers to ecosystem's stability and capability of tolerating disturbance and restoring itself. If the disturbance is of sufficient magnitude or duration, a threshold may be reached where the ecosystem changes state, possibly permanently. Sustainable use of environmental goods and services requires understanding and consideration of the resilience of the ecosystem and its limits. However, the elements which influence ecosystem resilience are complicated. For example various elements such as the water cycle, fertility, biodiversity, plant diversity and climate, interact fiercely and effect different systems.

There are many areas where human activity impacts upon and is also dependent upon the resilience of terrestrial, aquatic and marine ecosystems. These include agriculture, deforestation, pollution, mining, recreation, overfishing, dumping of waste into the sea and climate change.

Agriculture

Agriculture can be seen as a significant example which the resilience of terrestrial ecosystems should be considered. The organic matter (elements carbon and nitrogen) in soil, which is supposed to be recharged by multiple plants, is the main source of nutrients for crop growth . At the same time, intensive agriculture practices in response to global food demand and shortages involves the removal of weeds and the application of fertilisers to increase food production. However as a result of agricultural intensification and the application of herbicides to control weeds, fertilisers to accelerate and increase crop growth and pesticides to control insects, plant biodiversity is reduced as is the supply of organic matter to replenish soil nutrients and prevent run-off. This leads to a reduction in soil fertility and productivity. More sustainable agricultural practices would take into account and estimate the resilience of the land and monitor and balance the input and output of organic matter.

Deforestation

The term deforestation has a meaning that covers crossing the threshold of forest's resilience and losing its ability to return its originally stable state.

To recover itself, a forest ecosystem needs suitable interactions among climate conditions and bio-actions, and enough area. In addition, generally, the resilience of a forest system allows recovery from a relatively small scale of damage (such as lightning or landslide) of up to 10 per cent of its area . The larger the scale of damage, the more difficult it is for the forest ecosystem to restore and maintain its balance.

Deforestation also decreases biodiversity of both plant and animal life and can lead to an alteration of the climatic conditions of an entire area. Deforestation can also lead to species extinction, which can have a domino effect particularly when keystone species are removed or when a significant number of species is removed and their ecological function is lost.

Climate Change

Climate change is threatening coastal communities in a variety of ways such as rising sea levels, increasingly frequent large storms, tidal surges and flooding damage. One of the main results of climate change is rising sea water temperature which seriously effect on coral reefs through thermal-stress related coral bleaching. Between 1997-1998 the most significant worldwide coral bleaching event was recorded which corresponded with the El Nino Southern Oscillation, with significant damage to the coral reefs of the Western Indian Ocean.

Overfishing

It has been estimated by the United Nations Food and Agriculture Organisation that over 70 per cent of the world's fish stocks are either fully exploited or depleted which means overfishing threatens marine ecosystem resilience and this is mostly by rapid growth of fishing technology . One of the negative effects on marine ecosystems is that over the last half-century the stocks of coastal fish have had a huge reduction as a result of over-fishing for its economic benefits. Blue fin tuna is at particular risk of extinction. Depletion of fish stocks results in lowered biodiversity and consequently imbalance in the food chain, and increased vulnerability to disease.

In addition to overfishing, coastal communities are suffering the impacts of growing numbers of large commercial fishing vessels in causing reductions of small local fishing fleets. Many local lowland rivers which are sources of fresh water have become degraded because of the inflows of pollutants and sediments.

Dumping of Waste into the Sea

Dumping both depends upon ecosystem resilience whilst threatening it. Dumping of sewage and other contaminants into the ocean is often undertaken for the dispersive nature of the oceans and adaptive nature and ability for marine life to process the marine debris and contaminants. However, waste dumping threatens marine ecosystems by poisoning marine life and eutrophication.

Poisoning Marine Life

According to the International Maritime Organisation oil spills can have serious effects on marine life. The OILPOL Convention recognized that most oil pollution resulted from routine shipboard operations such as the cleaning of cargo tanks. In the 1950s, the normal practice was simply to wash the tanks out with water and then pump the resulting mixture of oil and water into the sea. OILPOL 54 prohibited the dumping of oily wastes within a certain distance from land and in 'special areas' where the danger to the environment was especially acute. In 1962 the limits were extended by means of an amendment adopted at a conference organized by IMO. Meanwhile, IMO in 1965 set up a Subcommittee on Oil Pollution, under the auspices of its Maritime Safety committee, to address oil pollution issues.

The threat of oil spills to marine life is recognised by those likely to be responsible for the pollution, such as the International Tanker Owners Pollution Federation.

The marine ecosystem is highly complex and natural fluctuations in species composition, abundance and distribution are a basic feature of its normal function. The extent of damage can therefore be difficult to detect against this background variability. Nevertheless, the key to understanding damage and its importance is whether spill effects result in a downturn in breeding success, productivity, diversity and the overall functioning of the system. Spills are not the only pressure on marine habitats; chronic urban and industrial contamination or the exploitation of the resources they provide are also serious threats.

Eutrophication and Algal Blooms

The Woods Hole Oceanographic Institution calls nutrient pollution the most widespread, chronic environmental problem in the coastal ocean. The discharges of nitrogen, phosphorus, and other nutrients come from agriculture, waste disposal, coastal development, and fossil fuel use. Once nutrient pollution reaches the coastal zone, it stimulates harmful overgrowths of algae, which can have direct toxic effects and ultimately result in low-oxygen conditions. Certain types of algae are toxic. Overgrowths of these algae result in harmful algal blooms, which are more colloquially referred to as 'red tides' or 'brown tides'. Zooplankton eat the toxic algae and begin passing the toxins up the food chain, affecting edibles like clams, and ultimately working their way up to seabirds, marine mammals, and humans. The result can be illness and sometimes death.

Resilience and Environmental Management

Ecological resilience and the thresholds by which resilience is defined are closely interrelated in the way that they influence environmental policy-making, legislation and subsequently environmental management. The ability of ecosystems to recover from certain levels of environmental impact is not explicitly noted in legislation, however, because of ecosystem resilience, some levels of environmental impact associated with development are made permissible by environmental policy-making and ensuing legislation.

Some examples of the consideration of ecosystem resilience within legislation include:

- *Environmental Planning and Assessment Act 1979* (NSW) — A key goal of the Environmental Assessment procedure is to determine whether proposed development will have a significant impact upon ecosystems.
- *Protection of the Environment (Operations) Act 1997* (NSW) — Pollution control is dependent upon keeping levels of pollutants emitted by industrial and other human activities below levels which would be harmful to the environment and its ecosystems. Environmental protection licenses are administered to maintain the environmental objectives of the POEO Act and breaches of licence conditions can attract heavy penalties and in some cases criminal convictions.
- *Threatened Species Conservation Act 1995* (NSW) — This Act seeks to protect threatened species while balancing it with development.

There is increasing awareness that greater understanding of the ecosystem resilience is required to reach the goal of sustainable development . Scientific research associated with resilience is beginning to play a role in influencing policy-making and subsequent environmental decision making.

This occurs in a number of ways:

- Observed resilience within specific ecosystems drives management practice. When resilience is observed to be low, or impact seems to be reaching the threshold, management response can be to alter human behaviour to result in less adverse impact to the ecosystem
- Ecosystem resilience impacts upon the way that development is permitted/environmental decision making is undertaken, similar to the way that existing ecosystem health impacts upon what development is permitted. For instance, remnant vegetation in the states of Queensland and New South Wales are classified in terms of ecosystem health and abundance. Any impact that development has upon threatened ecosystems must consider the health and resilience of these ecosystems. This is governed by the *Threatened Species Conservation Act 1995* in New South Wales and the *Vegetation Management Act 1999* in Queensland.

- International level initiatives aim at improving socio-ecological resilience worldwide through the cooperation and contributions of scientific and other experts. An example of such an initiative is the Millenium Ecosystem Assessment whose objective is "to assess the consequences of ecosystem change for human well-being and the scientific basis for action needed to enhance the conservation and sustainable use of those systems and their contribution to human well-being". Similarly, the United Nations Environment Programme aim is "to provide leadership and encourage partnership in caring for the environment by inspiring, informing, and enabling nations and peoples to improve their quality of life without compromising that of future generations. .

CHAPTER 9

Ecological Stability

Ecological stability can refer to types of stability in a continuum ranging from resilience (returning quickly to a previous state) to constancy to persistence. The precise definition depends on the ecosystem in question, the variable or variables of interest, and the overall context. In the context of conservation ecology, stable populations are often defined as ones that do not go extinct. Researchers applying mathematical models from system dynamics usually use Lyapunov stability.

Local stability indicates that a system is stable over small short-lived disturbances, while global stability indicates a system highly resistant to change in species composition and/or food web dynamics.

Observational studies of ecosystems use constancy to describe living systems that can remain unchanged.

Resistance and *inertia* deal with a system's inherent response to some perturbation.

A perturbation is any externally imposed change in conditions, usually happening in a short time period. Resistance is a measure of how little the variable of interest changes in response to external pressures. Inertia (or persistence) implies that the living system is able to resist external fluctuations. In the context of changing ecosystems in post-glacial North America, E.C. Pielou remarked at the outset of her overview.

"It obviously takes considerable time for mature vegetation to become established on newly exposed ice scoured rocks or glacial till...it also takes considerable time for whole ecosystems to change, with their numerous interdependent plant species, the habitats these create, and the animals that live in the habitats. Therefore, climatically caused fluctuations in ecological communities are a damped, smoothed-out version of the climatic fluctuations that cause them".

Resilience, Elasticity and Amplitude

Resilience is the tendency of a system to return to a previous state after a perturbation. *Elasticity* and *amplitude* are measures of resilience. Elasticity is the speed with which a system returns. Amplitude is a measure of how far a system can be moved from the previous state and still return. Ecology borrows the idea of neighborhood stability and a domain of attraction from dynamical systems theory.

Ecosystem

An ecosystem is a biological environment consisting of all the organisms living in a particular area, as well as all the non-living, physical components of the environment with which the organisms interact, such as air, soil, water, and sunlight. It is all the organisms in a given area, along with the non-living (abiotic) factors with which they interact; a biological community and its physical environment.

The entire array of organisms inhabiting a particular ecosystem is called a community. In a typical ecosystem, plants and other photosynthetic organisms are the producers that provide the food. Ecosystems can be permanent or temporary. Ecosystems usually form a number of food webs.

Ecosystems are functional units consisting of living things in a given area, non-living chemical and physical factors of their environment, linked together through nutrient cycle and energy flow.

- Natural
- Terrestrial ecosystem
- Aquatic ecosystem
- Lentic, the ecosystem of a lake, pond or swamp
- Lotic, the ecosystem of a river, stream or spring
- Artificial, environments created by humans

Central to the ecosystem concept is the idea that living organisms interact with every other element in their local environment. Eugene Odum, a founder of ecology, stated: "Any unit that includes all of the organisms (ie: the 'community') in a given area interacting with the physical environment so that a flow of energy leads to clearly defined trophic structure, biotic diversity, and material cycles (i.e.: exchange of materials between living and nonliving parts) within the system is an ecosystem".

Etymology

The term ecosystem was coined in 1930 by Roy Clapham to mean the combined physical and biological components of an environment. British ecologist Arthur Tansley later refined the term, describing it as "The whole system, . . . including not only the organism-complex, but also the whole complex of physical factors forming what we call the environment". Tansley regarded ecosystems not simply as natural units, but as mental isolates. Tansley later defined the spatial extent of ecosystems using the term ecotope.

Biomes

Biomes are a classification of globally similar areas, including ecosystems, such as ecological communities of plants and animals, soil organisms and climatic conditions. Biomes are in part defined based on factors such as plant structures (such as trees, shrubs and grasses), leaf types (such as broadleaf and needleleaf), plant spacing (forest, woodland, savanna) and climate. Unlike ecozones, biomes are not defined by genetic, taxonomic or historical similarities. Biomes are often identified with particular patterns of ecological succession and climax vegetation.

A fundamental classification of biomes is:

- Terrestrial (land) biomes.
- Freshwater biomes.
- Marine biomes.

Ecosystems have become particularly important politically, since the Convention on Biological Diversity (CBD) — ratified by 192 countries — defines "the protection of ecosystems, natural habitats and the maintenance of viable populations of species in natural surroundings" as a commitment of ratifying countries. This has created the political necessity to spatially identify ecosystems and somehow distinguish among them. The CBD defines an 'ecosystem' as a "dynamic complex of plant, animal and micro-organism communities and their non-living environment interacting as a functional unit".

With the need of protecting ecosystems, the political need arose to describe and identify them efficiently. Vreugdenhil et al. argued that this could be achieved most effectively by using a physiognomic-ecological classification system, as ecosystems are easily recognizable in the field as well as on satellite images. They argued that the structure and seasonality of the associated vegetation, or flora, complemented with ecological data (such as elevation, humidity, and drainage), are each determining modifiers that separate partially distinct sets of species. This is true not only for plant species, but also for species of animals, fungi and bacteria. The degree of ecosystem distinction is subject to the physiognomic modifiers that can be identified on an image and/or in the field. Where necessary, specific fauna elements can be added, such as seasonal concentrations of animals and the distribution of coral reefs.

Several physiognomic-ecological classification systems are available:

- Physiognomic-Ecological Classification of Plant Formations of the Earth: a system based on the 1974 work of Mueller-Dombois and Heinz Ellenberg, and developed by UNESCO. This classificatie "describes the above-ground or underwater vegetation structures and cover as observed in the field, described as plant life forms. This classification is fundamentally a species-independent physiognomic, hierarchical vegetation classification system which also takes into account ecological factors such as climate, elevation, human influences such as grazing, hydric regimes and survival strategies such as seasonality. The system was expanded with a basic classification for open water formations".
- Land Cover Classification System (LCCS), developed by the Food and Agriculture Organization (FAO).
- Forest-Range Environmental Study Ecosystems (FRES) developed by the United States Forest Service for use in the United States.

Several aquatic classification systems are available, and an effort is being made by the United States Geological Survey (USGS) and the Inter-American Biodiversity Information Network (IABIN) to design a complete ecosystem classification system that will cover both terrestrial and aquatic ecosystems.

From a philosophy of science perspective, ecosystems are not discrete units of nature that simply can be identified using the most 'correct' type of classification approach. In agreement with the definition by Tansley ('mental isolates'), any attempt to delineate or classify ecosystems should be explicit about the observer/analyst input in the classification including its normative rationale.

Two Giant Sequoias, Sequoia National Park. Note the large fire scar at the base of the right-hand tree; fires do not kill the trees but do remove competing thin-barked species, and aid Giant Sequoia regeneration.

Ecosystem Services

Ecosystem services are "fundamental life-support services upon which human civilization depends", and can be direct or indirect. Examples of direct ecosystem services are: pollination, wood and erosion prevention. Indirect services could be considered climate moderation, nutrient cycles and detoxifying natural substances.

The services and goods an ecosystem provides are often undervalued as many of them are without market value. Broad examples include:

- regulating (climate, floods, nutrient balance, water filtration)
- provisioning (food, medicine, fur)

- cultural (science, spiritual, ceremonial, recreation, aesthetic)
- supporting (nutrient cycling, photosynthesis, soil formation)

Ecosystem Legal Rights

Ecuador's new constitution of 2008 is the first in the world to recognize legally enforceable Rights of Nature, or ecosystem rights.

The borough of Tamaqua, Pennsylvania passed a law giving ecosystems legal rights. The ordinance establishes that the municipal government or any Tamaqua resident can file a lawsuit on behalf of the local ecosystem. Other townships, such as Rush, followed suit and passed their own laws.

This is part of a growing body of legal opinion proposing 'wild law'. Wild law, a term coined by Cormac Cullinan (a lawyer based in South Africa), would cover birds and animals, rivers and deserts.

From an anthropocentric point of view, some people perceive ecosystems as production units that produce goods and services, such as wood by forest ecosystems and grass for cattle by natural grasslands. Meat from wild animals, often referred to as bush meat in Africa, has proven to be extremely successful under well-controlled management schemes in South Africa and Kenya. Much less successful has been the discovery and commercialization of substances of wild organism for pharmaceutical purposes. Services derived from ecosystems are referred to as ecosystem services. They may include:

- facilitating the enjoyment of nature, which may generate many forms of income and employment in the tourism sector, often referred to as eco-tourisms;
- water retention, thus facilitating a more evenly distributed release of water;
- soil protection, open-air laboratory for scientific research, etc.

A greater degree of species or biological diversity — commonly referred to as Biodiversity — of an ecosystem may contribute to greater resilience of an ecosystem, because there are more species present at a location to respond to change and thus 'absorb' or reduce its effects. This reduces the effect before the ecosystem's structure is fundamentally changed to a different state. This is not universally the case and there is no proven relationship between the species diversity of an ecosystem and its ability to provide goods and services on a sustainable level: Humid tropical forests produce very few goods and direct services and are extremely vulnerable to change, while many temperate forests readily grow back to their previous state of development within a lifetime after felling or a forest fire. Some grasslands have been sustainably exploited for thousands of years (Mongolia, Africa, European peat and mooreland communities).

Introduction of new elements, whether biotic or abiotic, into an ecosystem tend to have a disruptive effect. In some cases, this can lead to ecological collapse or 'trophic cascading' and the death of many species within the ecosystem. Under this deterministic vision, the abstract notion of ecological health attempts to measure the robustness and recovery capacity for an ecosystem; i.e. how far the ecosystem is away from its steady state.

Often, however, ecosystems have the ability to rebound from a disruptive agent. The difference between collapse or a gentle rebound is determined by two factors–the toxicity of the introduced element and the resiliency of the original ecosystem.

Ecosystems are primarily governed by stochastic (chance) events, the reactions these events provoke on non-living materials and the responses by organisms to the conditions surrounding them. Thus, an ecosystem results from the sum of individual responses of organisms to stimuli from elements in the environment. The presence or absence of populations merely depends on reproductive and dispersal success, and population levels fluctuate in response to stochastic events. As the number of species in an ecosystem is higher, the number of stimuli is also higher. Since the beginning of life organisms have survived continuous change through natural selection of successful feeding, reproductive and dispersal behaviour. Through natural selection the planet's species have continuously adapted to change through variation in their biological composition and distribution. Mathematically it can be demonstrated that greater numbers of different interacting factors tend to dampen fluctuations in each of the individual factors.

Given the great diversity among organisms on earth, most ecosystems only changed very gradually, as some species would disappear while others would move in. Locally, sub-populations continuously go extinct, to be replaced later through dispersal of other sub-populations. Stochastists do recognize that certain intrinsic regulating mechanisms occur in nature. Feedback and response mechanisms at the species level regulate population levels, most notably through territorial behaviour. Andrewatha and Birch suggest that territorial behaviour tends to keep populations at levels where food supply is not a limiting factor. Hence, stochastists see territorial behaviour as a regulatory mechanism at the species level but not at the ecosystem level. Thus, in their vision, ecosystems are not regulated by feedback and response mechanisms from the (eco)system itself and there is no such thing as a balance of nature.

If ecosystems are governed primarily by stochastic processes, through which its subsequent state would be determined by both predictable and random actions, they may be more resilient to sudden change than each species individually. In the absence of a balance of nature, the species composition of ecosystems would undergo shifts that would depend on the nature of the change, but entire.

The theoretical ecologist Robert Ulanowicz has used information theory tools to describe the structure of ecosystems, emphasizing mutual information (correlations) in studied systems. Drawing on this methodology and prior observations of complex ecosystems, Ulanowicz depicts approaches to determining the stress levels on ecosystems and predicting system reactions to defined types of alteration in their settings (such as increased or reduced energy flow, and eutrophication.

In addition, Eric Sanderson has developed the Muir web, based on experience on the Mannahatta project. This graphical schematic shows how different species are connected to each other, not only regarding their position in the food chain, but also regarding other services, i.e. provisioning of shelter.

Ecosystem Ecology

Ecosystem ecology is the integrated study of biotic and abiotic components of ecosystems and their interactions within an ecosystem framework. This science examines how ecosystems work and relates this to their components such as chemicals, bedrock, soil, plants, and animals. Ecosystem ecology examines physical and biological structure and examines how these ecosystem characteristics interact.

CHAPTER 10

Community (Ecology)

In ecology, a community is an assemblage of two or more populations of different species occupying the same geographical area. The term community has a variety of uses. In its simplest form it refers to groups of organisms in a specific place and/or time, for example, "the fish community of Lake Ontario before industrialization".

Community ecologists study the interactions between species in communities on many spatial and temporal scales, including the distribution, structure, abundance, demography, and interactions between coexisting populations. The primary focus of community ecology is on the interactions between populations as determined by specific genotypic and phenotypic characteristics. Community ecology has its origin in European plant sociology. Modern community ecology examines patterns such as variation in species richness, equitability, productivity and food web structure (see community structure; it also examines processes such as predator-prey population dynamics, succession, and community assembly.

On a deeper level the meaning and value of the community concept in ecology is up for debate. Communities have traditionally been understood on a fine scale in terms of local processes constructing (or destructing) an assemblage of species, such as the way climate change is likely to affect the make-up of grass communities. Recently this local community focus has been criticised. Robert Ricklefs has argued that it's more useful to think of communities on a regional scale, drawing on evolutionary taxonomy and biogeography, where some species or clades evolve and others go extinct.

Competition

Species can compete with each other for finite resources. It is considered to be an important limiting factor of population size, biomass and species richness. Many types of competition have been described, but proving the existence of these interactions is a matter of debate. Direct competition has been observed between individuals, populations and species, but there is little evidence that competition has been the driving force in the evolution of large groups. For example, between amphibians, reptiles and mammals.

Interference competition: occurs when one population attacks, or consumes the resources, of another. Examples include a lion chasing a hyena from a kill, or a plant releasing allelopathic chemicals to impede the growth of a competing species.

Exploitative competition: occurs via the consumption of resources. When an individual of one species consumes a resource (e.g., food, shelter, sunlight, etc.), that resource is no longer available to be consumed by a member of a second species. Exploitative competition is thought to be more common in nature, but care must be taken to distinguish it from apparent competition.

Apparent competition: occurs when two species share a predator. The populations of both species can be depressed by predation without direct exploitative competition.

Predation

Predation is hunting another species for food. This is a positive-negative (+ -) interaction in that the predator species benefits while the prey species is harmed. Some predators kill their prey before eating them (e.g., a hawk killing a mouse). Other predators are parasites that feed on prey while alive (e.g., a vampire bat feeding on a cow). Herbivores feed on plants (e.g., a cow grazing). Predation may affect the population size of predators and prey and the number of species coexisting in a community.

Mutualism

Mutualism is a symbiotic interaction between species in which both benefit, and is thus a double positive (+ +) interaction. Examples include Rhizobium bacteria growing in nodules on the roots of legume plants and insects pollinating the flowers of angiosperms.

Community Structure

A major research theme among community ecology has been whether ecological communities have a (non-random) structure and, if so, how to characterise this structure. Forms of community structure include aggregation and nestedness.

In the study of complex networks, a network is said to have community structure if it divides naturally into groups of nodes with dense connections within groups and sparser connections between groups.

In the study of networks, such as computer and information networks, social networks or biological networks, a number of different characteristics have been found to occur commonly, including the small-world property, heavy-tailed degree distributions, and clustering, among others. Another common characteristic is community structure.

In the context of networks, community structure refers to the occurrence of groups of nodes in a network that are more densely connected internally than with the rest of the network, as shown in the example image to the right. This inhomogeneity of connections suggests that the network has certain natural divisions within it.

Not all networks need display community structure. Many model networks, for example, such as the random graph and the Barabási–Albert model, do not display community structure.

Why are We Interested In It?

Community structures are quite common in real networks. Social networks often include community groups (the origin of the term, in fact) based on common location, interests, occupation, etc. Metabolic networks have communities based on functional groupings. Citation networks form communities by research topic. Being able to identify these sub-structures within a network can provide insight into how network function and topology affect each other.

Algorithms for Finding Communities

Finding communities within an arbitrary network can be a difficult task. The number of communities, if any, within the network is typically unknown and the communities are often of unequal size and/or density. Despite these difficulties, however, several methods for community finding have been developed and employed with varying levels of success.

Minimum-cut Method

One of the oldest algorithms for dividing networks into parts is the minimum-cut method (and variants such as ratio cut and normalized cut). This method sees use, for example, in load balancing for parallel computing in order to minimize communication between processor nodes.

In the minimum-cut method, the network is divided into a predetermined number of parts, usually of approximately the same size, chosen such that the number of edges between groups is minimized. The method works well in many of the applications for which it was originally intended but is less than ideal for finding community structure in general networks since it will find communities regardless of whether they are implicit in the structure, and it will find only a fixed number of them.

Hierarchical Clustering

Another method for finding community structures in networks is hierarchical clustering. In this method one defines a similarity measure quantifying some (usually topological) type of similarity between node pairs. Commonly used measures include the cosine similarity, the Jaccard index, and the Hamming distance between rows of the adjacency matrix. Then one groups similar nodes into communities according to this measure. There are several common schemes for performing the grouping, the two simplest being single-linkage clustering, in which two groups are considered separate communities if and only if all pairs of nodes in different groups have similarity lower than a given threshold, and complete linkage clustering, in which all nodes within every group have similarity greater than threshold.

Girvan—Newman Algorithm

Another commonly used algorithm for finding communities is the Girvan–Newman algorithm . This algorithm identifies edges in a network that lie between communities and then removes them, leaving behind just the communities themselves. The identification is performed by employing the graph-theoretic measure betweenness, which assigns a number to each edge which is large if the edge lies 'between' many pairs of nodes.

The Girvan–Newman algorithm returns results of reasonable quality and is popular because it has been implemented in a number of standard software packages. But it also runs slowly, taking time $O(m^2n)$ on a network of n vertices and m edges, making it impractical for networks of more than a few thousand nodes.

Modularity Maximization

One of the most widely used methods for community detection is modularity maximization. Modularity is a benefit function that measures the quality of a particular division of a network into communities. The modularity maximization method detects communities by searching over possible divisions of a network for one or more that have particularly high modularity. Since exhaustive search over all possible divisions is usually intractable, practical algorithms are based on approximate optimization methods such as greedy algorithms, simulated annealing, or spectral optimization, with different approaches offering different balances between speed and accuracy. The usefulness of modularity optimization is however questionable: on the one hand, it has been shown that modularity optimization often fails to detect clusters smaller than some scale, depending on the size of the network (resolution limit); on the other hand the landscape of modularity values is characterized by a huge degeneracy of partitions with high modularity, close to the absolute maximum, which may be very different from each other.

Clique Percolation Method (CPM)

An algorithm for finding overlapping communities is provided by the clique percolation method. In this approach the communities are defined as percolation clusters of *k*-cliques. A *k*-clique is a complete sub-graph of *k*-nodes, two *k*-cliques are adjacent if they share *k* - 1 nodes, and a community corresponds to a maximal union of *k*-cliques in which we can reach any *k*-clique from any other *k*-clique through series of *k*-clique adjacencies. Since a node can belong to several different *k*-clique percolation clusters at the same time, the communities can overlap with each other.

Testing Methods of Finding Communities Algorithms

Most research on community detection has been concerned with the development of new methods and relatively little attention has been paid to the testing of those methods, i.e., to checking how good their performance is compared with other methods. To the extent that testing has taken place, a number of approaches have been employed. For instance, researchers have compared the modularity values of different algorithms applied to the same networks to see which algorithms find the community structures with highest modularity. Another approach involves applying algorithms to networks that have known community structure, to see whether that structure can be recovered. A number of real-world networks have become standard benchmarks for such problems, particularly the so-called 'karate club' network, a social network drawn from a well-known study of university students in the 1970s, and the 'college football' network, a network of American football games between US universities. Real-world networks have the advantage of presenting realistic challenges to algorithms, but the disadvantage that the nature and difficulty of those challenges cannot easily be controlled by the experimenter. An alternative approach is to use a computer-generated network that has community structure deliberately placed in it by the experimenter. A common example of this approach is the 'four groups' test, in which a network is divided into four equally-sized groups (usually of 32 nodes each) and the probabilities of connection within and between groups varied to create more or less challenging structures for the detection algorithm. Such benchmark graphs are a special case of the planted l-partition model of Condon and Karp, or more generally of 'stochastic block models', a general class of random network models containing community structure. Recently, other more flexible benchmarks have been proposed that allow for varying group sizes and non-trivial degree distributions, such as the benchmark of Lancichinetti *et. al.* , which is an extension of the four groups benchmark that includes heterogeneous distributions of node degree and community size, making it a more severe test of community detection methods.

CHAPTER 11

Ecological Niche

In ecology, a niche is a term describing the relational position of a species or population in its ecosystem to each other; e.g. a dolphin could potentially be in another ecological niche from one that travels in a different pod if the members of these pods utilize significantly different food resources and foraging methods. A shorthand definition of niche is how an organism makes a living. The ecological niche describes how an organism or population responds to the distribution of resources and competitors (e.g., by growing when resources are abundant, and when predators, parasites and pathogens are scarce) and how it in turn alters those same factors (e.g., limiting access to resources by other organisms, acting as a food source for predators and a consumer of prey).

The word 'niche' is derived from the Middle French word *nicher*, meaning *to nest*. The term was coined by the naturalist Joseph Grinnell in 1917, in his paper "The niche relationships of the California Thrasher." The Grinnelian niche concept embodies the idea that the niche of a species is determined by the habitat in which is lives in. In other words, the niche is the sum of the habitat requirements that allow a species to persist and produce offspring. For example, the behaviour of the California Thrasher is consistent with the chaparral habitat it lives in—it breeds and feeds in the underbrush; and escapes from predators by shuffling from underbrush to underbrush.

This perspective of niche allows for the existence of ecological equivalents and also empty niches. For example, the anolis lizards of the Greater Antilles are a rare example of convergent evolution, adaptive radiation, and the existence of ecological equivalents—the anolis lizards evolved in similar microhabitats independently of each other and resulted in the same ecomorphs across all four islands.

Eltonian Niche

In 1927 Charles Sutherland Elton, a British ecologist, gave the first working definition of the niche concept. He is credited with saying: "[W]hen an ecologist says 'there goes a badger,' he should include in his thoughts some definite idea of the animal's place in the community to which it belongs, just as if he had said, 'there goes the vicar".

The Eltonian niche encompasses the idea that the niche is the role a species plays in a community, rather than a habitat.

Hutchinsonian Niche

The Hutchinsonian Niche views niche as an n-dimensional hypervolume, where the dimensions are environmental conditions that define the range in which a species can persist.

The niche concept was popularized by the zoologist G. Evelyn Hutchinson in 1957. Hutchinson wanted to know why there are so many different types of organisms in any one habitat.

The full range of environmental conditions (biological and physical) under which an organism can exist describes its fundamental niche. As a result of pressure from, and interactions with, other organisms (e.g. superior competitors), species are usually forced to occupy a niche that is narrower than this, and to which they are mostly highly adapted. This is termed the realized niche. The ecological niche has also been termed by G.E. Hutchinson a 'hypervolume'. This term defines the multi-dimensional space of resources (e.g., light, nutrients, structure, etc.) available to (and specifically used by) organisms. The term adaptive zone was coined by the paleontologist, George Gaylord Simpson, and refers to a set of ecological niches that may be occupied by a group of species that exploit the same resources in a similar manner.

Hutchinson's 'niche' (a description of the ecological space occupied by a species) is subtly different from the 'niche' as defined by Grinnell (an ecological role, that may or may not be actually filled by a species–see vacant niches).

Different species cannot occupy the same niche (or guild). A niche is a very specific segment of ecospace occupied by a single species. Species can however share a 'mode of life' or 'autecological strategy' which are broader definitions of ecospace. For example, Australian grasslands species, though different from those of the Great Plains grasslands, occupy the similar modes of life.

Once a niche is left vacant, other organisms can fill that position. For example, the niche that was left vacant by the extinction of the tarpan has been filled by other animals (in particular a small horse breed, the konik).

Also, when plants and animals are introduced into a new environment, they have the potential to occupy or invade the niche or niches of native organisms, often outcompeting the indigenous species. Introduction of non-indigenous species to non-native habitats by humans often results in biological pollution by the exotic or invasive species.

The mathematical representation of a species' fundamental niche in ecological space, and its subsequent projection back into geographic space, is the domain of niche modelling.

The different dimensions, or plot axes, of a niche represent different biotic and abiotic variables. These factors may include descriptions of the organism's life history, habitat, trophic position (place in the food chain), and geographic range. According to the competitive exclusion principle, no two species can occupy the same niche in the same environment for a long time.

Culling

Culling is the process of removing animals from a group based on specific criteria. This is done in order to either reinforce certain desirable characteristics or to remove certain undesirable characteristics from the group. For livestock and wildlife, the process of culling usually implies the killing of animals with undesirable characteristics.

The word comes from the Latin colligere, which means collect. The term can be applied broadly to mean sorting a collection into two groups: one that will be kept and one that will be rejected. The cull is the set of items rejected during the selection process. For example, if you were to cull a collection of marbles such that only red marbles are chosen, the cull would be the set of marbles that are not red. In this example, the selection process would be culling on red marbles. The implicit meaning is that the cull (the non-red marbles) are going to be the group rejected.

The culling process is repeated until the selected group is of proper size and consistency desired. Take for example a talent contest. During the first round all the contestants compete and are evaluated. Since only a limited number of the contestants can continue to the next round of the competition, the group is culled based on the judge's opinions. Those contestants that are not selected to continue are culled from the group. During the second round, the contestants perform again, have their performances judged, and are culled again based on the judges scoring. This process continues until the finalists and eventually the winner of the contest is chosen. By repeating the selection criteria with more stringent criteria on each round of the competition, the judges are able to cull the group to the single individual that they felt performed the best during the competition.

Pedigreed Animals

Culling: The rejection or removal of inferior individuals from breeding. The act of selective breeding. As used in the practice of breeding pedigree cats, this refers to the practice of spaying or neutering a kitten or cat that does not measure up to the show standard (or other standard being applied) for that breed. In no way does culling, as used by responsible breeders, signify the killing of healthy kittens or cats if they fail to meet the applicable standard."

—*Robinson's Genetics for Cat Breeders and Veterinarians,* Fourth Edition

In the breeding of pedigreed animals, both desirable and undesirable traits are considered when choosing which animals to retain for breeding and which to place as pets. The process of culling starts with examination of the conformation standard of the animal and will often include additional qualities such as health, robustness, temperament, colour preference, etc. The breeder takes all things into consideration when envisioning his/her ideal for the breed or goal of their breeding programme. From that vision, selections are made as to which animals, when bred, have the best chance of producing the ideal for the breed.

Breeders of pedigreed animals cull based on many criteria. The first culling criteria should always be health and robustness. Secondary to health, temperament and conformation of the animal should be considered. The filtering process ending with the breeders personal preferences on pattern, colour, etc.

The Tandem Method

The Tandem Method is a form of selective breeding where a breeder addresses one characteristic of the animal at a time. Thus selecting only animals that measure above a certain threshold for that particular trait while keeping other traits constant. Once that level of quality in the single trait is achieved, the breeder will focus on a second trait and cull based on that quality. With the tandem method, a minimum level of quality is set for important characteristics that the breeder wishes to remain constant. The breeder is focussing improvement in one particular trait without losing quality of the others. The breeder will raise the threshold for selection on this trait with each successive generation of progeny. Thus insuring improvement in this single characteristic of her breeding programme.

For example, lets say that a breeder is pleased with the muzzle length, muzzle shape, and eye placement in her breeding stock, but wishes to improve the eye shape of progeny produced. The breeder then determines a minimum level of improvement in eye shape required for her to fold progeny back into her breeding programme. Progeny is first evaluated on the existing quality thresholds in place for muzzle length, muzzle shape, and eye placement with the additional criteria being improvement in eye shape. Any animal that does not meet this level of improvement in the eye shape while maintaining the other qualities is culled from the breeding programme. Meaning, that animal is not used for breeding, but rather is spayed/neutered and placed in a pet home.

Independent Levels

Independent levels is a method where any animal who falls below a given standard in any single characteristic is not used in a breeding programme. With each successive mating, the threshold culling criteria is raised thus improving the breed with each successive generation.

This method measures several characteristics at once. Should progeny fall below the desired quality in any one characteristic being measured, it will be not be used in the breeding programme regardless of the level of excellence of other traits. With each successive generation of progeny, the minimum quality of each characteristic is raised thus insuring improvement of these traits.

For example, a breeder has a view of what the minimum requirements for muzzle length, muzzle shape, eye placement, and eye shape she is breeding toward. The breeder will determine what the minimum acceptable quality for each of these traits will be for progeny to be folded back into her breeding programme. Any animal that fails to meet the quality threshold for any one of these criteria is culled from the breeding programme. Meaning, that animal is not used for breeding, but rather is spayed/neutered and placed in a pet home.

Total Score Method

The Total Score Method is a method where the breeder evaluates and selects breeding stock based on a weighted table of characteristics. The breeder selects qualities that are most important to them and assigns them a weight. The weights of all the traits should add up to 100. When evaluating an individual for selection, the breeder measures the traits on a scale of 1 to 10, with 10 being the most desirable expression and 1 being the lowest. The scores are then multiplied by their weights and then added together to give a total score. Individuals that fail to meet a threshold are culled (or removed) from the breeding programme. The total score gives a breeder a way to evaluate multiple traits on an animal at the same time.

The total score method is the most flexible of the three. it allows for weighted improvement of multiple characteristics. It allows the breeder to make major gains in one aspect while moderate or lesser gains in others.

For example, a breeder is willing to make a smaller improvement in muzzle length and muzzle shape in order to have a moderate gain in improvement of eye placement and a more dramatic improvement in eye shape. Suppose the breeder determines that she would like to see 40 per cent improvement in eye shape, 30 per cent improvement in eye placement, and 15 per cent improvement in both muzzle length and shape. The breeder would evaluate these characteristics on a scale of 1 to 10 and multiply by the weights. The formula would look something like: 15 (muzzle length) + 15(muzzle shape) + 30(eye placement) + 40(eye shape) = total score for that animal. The breeder determines the lowest acceptable total score for an animal to be folded back into their breeding programme. Animals that do not meet this minimum total score are culled from the breeding programme. Meaning, that animal is not used for breeding, but rather is spayed/neutered and placed in a pet home.

Livestock and Production Animals

Since livestock is bred for the production of meat or milk, the herd must be culled to a certain number of production or meat animals a farmer wishes to maintain. Animals not selected to remain for breeding are sent to the slaughter house, sold, or killed.

Criteria for culling livestock and production animals can be based on population or production (milk or egg). In a domestic or farming situation the culling process involves selection and the selling of surplus stock. The selection may be done to improve breeding stock, for example for improved production of eggs or milk, or simply to control the group's population for the benefit of the environment and other species.

With dairy cattle, culling may be practised by inseminating inferior cows with beef breed semen and by selling the produced offspring for meat production.

With poultry, males which would grow up to be roosters have little use in an industrial egg-producing facility. Approximately half of the newly hatched chicks will be male and would grow up to be roosters, which do not lay eggs. For this reason, the hatchlings are culled based on gender. Most of the male chicks are usually killed shortly after hatching.

Wildlife

In the United States, hunting licenses and hunting seasons are a means by which the population of game animals is maintained. Each season, a hunter is allowed to kill a certain amount of wild game. The amount is determined both by species and gender. If the population seems to have surplus females, hunters are allowed to take more females during that hunting season. If the population is below what is desired, hunters may not be permitted to hunt that particular game animal or only hunt a restricted number of males.

Populations of game animals such as elk may be informally culled if they begin to excessively eat winter food set out for domestic cattle herds. In such instances the rancher will inform hunters that they may "hunt the haystack" on his property in order to thin the wild herd to controllable levels. These efforts are aimed to counter excessive depletion of the intended 'domestic' winter feed supplies. Other managed culling instances involve extended issuance of extra hunting licenses, or the inclusion of additional 'special hunting seasons' during harsh winters or overpopulation periods, governed by state fish and game Agencies.

Culling for population control is common in wildlife management, particularly on African game farms and in Australia in national parks. In the case of very large animals such as elephants, adults are often targeted. Their orphaned young, easily captured and transported, are then relocated. Without proper elephant socialization, young male elephants are believed to become unruly and extremely dangerous to other elephants, wildlife and humans. Culling is controversial in many African countries, but reintroduction of the practice has been recommended in recent years for use at the Kruger National Park in South Africa, which has experienced a swell in its elephant population since culling was banned in 1995.

In fishing tournaments, culling refers to releasing smaller fish that won't be used to count towards an angler's total weight. For instance, if an angler is allowed to weigh in only 4 fish, he might keep his first four 2 pound fish in the livewell until he starts to catch bigger fish. As he catches bigger fish, he can release (or cull) the smaller fish.

In certain cases culling may also be undertaken to check outbreak of certain viral or other infections and diseases among animals or birds. This has become widespread in India and some other East Asian countries where there are outbreaks of the deadly Influenza A virus subtype H5N1 among poultry. Huge numbers of chickens and some other fowls are being culled (as of December 2008) in order to contain spread of the avian flu.

Culling would require a lot of safety steps to be maintained in such cases of culling animals/birds since even a minor fault can cause the infections to spread out from the affected animals/birds to the population at large. Safety measures may include wearing special protective clothing and breathing apparatus to keep the workers culling the affected animals/birds from getting infected.

Population Density

Population density (in agriculture standing stock and standing crop) is a measurement of population per unit area or unit volume. It is frequently applied to living organisms, and particularly to humans. It is a key geographic term.

Population density is population divided by total land area.

Low densities may cause an extinction vortex and lead to further reduced fertility. This is called the Allee effect after the scientist who identified it. Examples of the causes in low population densities include:

- Increased problems with locating mates
- Increased inbreeding

Different species have different expected densities. *R*-selected species commonly have high population densities, while *K*-selected species may have lower densities. Low densities may be associated with specialized mate location adaptations such as specialized pollinators; as found in the orchid family (*Orchidaceae*).

For humans, population density is the number of people per unit of area usually per square kilometre or mile (which may include or exclude cultivated or potentially productive area). Commonly this may be calculated for a county, city, country, another territory, or the entire world.

The world's population is 6.8 billion, and Earth's total area (including land and water) is 510 million square kilometres (197 million square miles). Therefore the worldwide human population density is 6.8 billion ÷ 510 million = 13.3 per km^2 (34.5 per sq. mile). If only the Earth's land area of 150 million km^2 (58 million sq. miles) is taken into account, then human population density increases to 45.3 per km^2 (117.2 per sq. mile). This calculation includes all continental and island land area, including Antarctica. If Antarctica is also excluded, then population density rises to 50 people per km^2 (129.28 per sq. mile). Considering that over half of the Earth's land mass consists of areas inhospitable to human inhabitation, such as deserts and high mountains, and that population tends to cluster around seaports and fresh water sources, this number by itself does not give any meaningful measurement of human population density.

Several of the most densely-populated territories in the world are city-states, microstates, micronations, or dependencies. These territories share a relatively small area and a high urbanization level, with an economically specialized city population drawing also on rural resources outside the area, illustrating the difference between high population density and overpopulation.

Cities with high population densities are, by some, considered to be overpopulated, though the extent to which this is the case depends on factors like quality of housing and infrastructure and access to resources. Most of the most densely-populated cities are in southern and eastern Asia, though Cairo and Lagos in Africa also fall into this category.

City population is, however, heavily dependent on the definition of 'urban area' used: densities are often higher for the central municipality itself, than when more recently-developed and administratively unincorporated suburban communities are included, as in the concepts of agglomeration or metropolitan area, the latter including sometimes neighbouring cities. For instance, Milwaukee has a greater population density when just the inner city is measured, and not the surrounding suburbs as well.

While arithmetic density is the most common way of measuring population density, several other methods have been developed which aim to provide a more accurate measure of population density over a specific area.

- *Arithmetic density:* The total number of people/area of land (measured in km^2 or sq miles).
- *Physiological density:* The total population/area of arable land.
- *Agricultural density:* The total rural population/area of agricultural land.
- *Residential density:* The number of people living in an urban area/area of residential land.
- *Urban density:* The number of people inhabiting an urban area / total area of urban land.

- *Ecological optimum:* The density of population which can be supported by the natural resources.

Organism

In biology, an organism is any contiguous living system (such as animal, plant, fungus, or micro-organism). In at least some form, all organisms are capable of response to stimuli, reproduction, growth and development, and maintenance of homoeostasis as a stable whole. An organism may either be unicellular (single-celled) or be composed of, as in humans, many trillions of cells grouped into specialized tissues and organs. The term *multicellular* (many-celled) describes any organism made up of more than one cell.

The term 'organism' (Greek — *organismos*, from Ancient Greek — *organon* 'organ, instrument, tool') first appeared in the English language in 1701 and took on its current definition by 1834 (Oxford English Dictionary).

Scientific classification in biology considers organisms synonymous with life on Earth. Based on cell type, organisms may be divided into the prokaryotic and eukaryotic groups. The prokaryotes represent two separate domains, the Bacteria and Archaea. Eukaryotic organisms, with a membrane-bounded cell nucleus, also contain organelles, namely mitochondria and (in plants) plastids, generally considered to be derived from endosymbiotic bacteria. Fungi, animals and plants are examples of species that are eukaryotes.

More recently a clade, Neomura, has been proposed, which groups together the Archaea and Eukarya. Neomura is thought to have evolved from Bacteria, more specifically from Actinobacteria.

The word *'organism'* may broadly be defined as *an assembly of molecules that function as a more or less stable whole and has the properties of life.* However, many sources propose definitions that exclude viruses and theoretically possible man-made non-organic life forms. Viruses are dependent on the biochemical machinery of a host cell for reproduction.

Chambers Online Reference provides a broad definition: "any living structure, such as a plant, animal, fungus or bacterium, capable of growth and reproduction".

In multicellular terms, 'organism' usually describes the whole hierarchical assemblage of systems (for example circulatory, digestive, or reproductive) themselves collections of organs; these are, in turn, collections of tissues, which are themselves made of cells. In some plants and the nematode *Caenorhabditis elegans*, individual cells are totipotent.

A superorganism is an organism consisting of many individuals working together as a single functional or social unit.

Viruses

Viruses are not typically considered to be organisms because they are incapable of 'independent' or autonomous reproduction or metabolism. This controversy is problematic because some cellular organisms are also incapable of independent survival (but not of independent metabolism and procreation) and live as obligatory intracellular parasites. Although viruses have a few enzymes and molecules characteristic of living organisms, they have no metabolism of their own and cannot synthesize and organize the organic compounds that form them. Naturally, this rules out autonomous reproduction and they can only be passively replicated by the machinery of the host cell. In this sense they are similar to inanimate matter. While viruses sustain no independent metabolism, and thus are usually not accounted organisms, they do have their own genes and they do evolve by similar mechanisms by which organisms evolve.

The hierarchy of biological classification's eight major taxonomic ranks, which is an example of definition by genus and differentia. Intermediate minor rankings are not shown.

All organisms are classified by the science of alpha taxonomy into either taxa or clades.

Taxa are ranked groups of organisms, which run from the general (domain) to the specific (species). A broad scheme of ranks in hierarchical order is:

- Domain
- Kingdom
- Phylum
- Class
- Order
- Family
- Genus
- Species

To give an example, *Homo sapiens* is the Latin binomial equating to modern humans. All members of the species *sapiens* are, at least in theory, genetically able to interbreed. Several species may belong to a genus, but the members of different species within a genus are unable to interbreed to produce fertile offspring. Homo, however, only has one surviving species (sapiens), *Homo erectus, Homo neanderthalensis,* etc. having become extinct thousands of years ago. Several genera belong to the same family and so on up the hierarchy. Eventually, the relevant kingdom (Animalia, in the case of humans) is placed into one of the three domains depending upon certain genetic and structural characteristics.

All living organisms known to science are given classification by this system such that the species within a particular family are more closely related and genetically similar than the species within a particular phylum.

Organisms are complex chemical systems, organized in ways that promote reproduction and some measure of sustainability or survival. The molecular phenomena of chemistry are fundamental in understanding organisms, but it is a philosophical error (reductionism) to reduce organismal biology to mere chemistry. It is generally the phenomena of entire organisms that determine their fitness to an environment and therefore the survivability of their DNA based genes.

Organisms clearly owe their origin, metabolism, and many other internal functions to chemical phenomena, especially the chemistry of large organic molecules. Organisms are complex systems of chemical compounds that, through interaction and environment, play a wide variety of roles.

Organisms are semi-closed chemical systems. Although they are individual units of life (as the definition requires) they are not closed to the environment around them. To operate they constantly take in and release energy. Autotrophs produce usable energy (in the form of organic compounds) using light from the sun or inorganic compounds while heterotrophs take in organic compounds from the environment.

The primary chemical element in these compounds is carbon. The physical properties of this element such as its great affinity for bonding with other small atoms, including other carbon atoms, and its small size make it capable of forming multiple bonds, make it ideal as the basis of organic life. It is able to form small three-atom compounds (such as carbon dioxide), as well as large chains of many thousands of atoms that can store data (nucleic acids), hold cells together, and transmit information (protein).

Macromolecules

Compounds that make up organisms may be divided into macromolecules and other, smaller molecules. The four groups of macromolecule are nucleic acids, proteins, carbohydrates and lipids. Nucleic acids (specifically deoxyribonucleic acid, or DNA) store genetic data as a sequence of nucleotides. The particular sequence of the four different types of nucleotides (adenine, cytosine, guanine, and thymine) dictate the many characteristics that constitute the organism. The sequence is divided up into codons, each of which is a particular sequence of three nucleotides and corresponds to a particular amino acid. Thus a sequence of DNA codes for a particular protein that, due to the chemical properties of the amino acids it is made from, folds in a particular manner and so performs a particular function.

These protein functions have been recognized:

- Enzymes, which catalyze all of the reactions of metabolism
- Structural proteins, such as tubulin, or collagen
- Regulatory proteins, such as transcription factors or cyclins that regulate the cell cycle
- Signaling molecules or their receptors such as some hormones and their receptors
- Defensive proteins, which can include everything from antibodies of the immune system, to toxins (e.g., dendrotoxins of snakes), to proteins that include unusual amino acids like canavanine.

Lipids make up the membrane of cells that constitutes a barrier, containing everything within the cell and preventing compounds from freely passing into, and out of, the cell. In some multicellular organisms they serve to store energy and mediate communication between cells. Carbohydrates also store and transport energy in some organisms, but are more easily broken down than lipids.

Structure

All organisms consist of monomeric units called cells; some contain a single cell (unicellular) and others contain many units (multicellular). Multicellular organisms are able to specialize cells to perform specific functions, a group of such cells is tissue the four basic types of which are epithelium, nervous tissue, muscle tissue, and connective tissue. Several types of tissue work together in the form of an organ to produce a particular function (such as the pumping of the blood by the heart, or as a barrier to the environment as the skin). This pattern continues to a higher level with several organs functioning as an organ system to allow for reproduction, digestion, etc. Many multicelled organisms consist of several organ systems, which coordinate to allow for life.

The Cell

The cell theory, first developed in 1839 by Schleiden and Schwann, states that all organisms are composed of one or more cells; all cells come from preexisting cells; all vital functions of an organism occur within cells, and cells contain the hereditary information necessary for regulating cell functions and for transmitting information to the next generation of cells.

There are two types of cells, eukaryotic and prokaryotic. Prokaryotic cells are usually singletons, while eukaryotic cells are usually found in multi-cellular organisms. Prokaryotic cells lack a nuclear membrane so DNA is unbound within the cell, eukaryotic cells have nuclear membranes.

All cells, whether prokaryotic or eukaryotic, have a membrane, which envelops the cell, separates its interior from its environment, regulates what moves in and out, and maintains the electric potential of the cell. Inside the membrane, a salty cytoplasm takes up most of the cell volume. All cells possess DNA, the hereditary material of genes, and RNA, containing the information necessary to build various proteins such as enzymes, the cell's primary machinery. There are also other kinds of biomolecules in cells.

All cells share several abilities:

- Reproduction by cell division (binary fission, mitosis or meiosis).
- Use of enzymes and other proteins coded for by DNA genes and made via messenger RNA intermediates and ribosomes.
- Metabolism, including taking in raw materials, building cell components, converting energy, molecules and releasing by-products. The functioning of a cell depends upon its ability to extract and use chemical energy stored in organic molecules. This energy is derived from metabolic pathways.
- Response to external and internal stimuli such as changes in temperature, pH or nutrient levels. Cell contents are contained within a cell surface membrane that contains proteins and a lipid bilayer.

In biology, the theory of universal common descent proposes that all organisms on Earth are descended from a common ancestor or ancestral gene pool. Evidence for common descent may be found in traits shared between all living organisms. In Darwin's day, the evidence of shared traits was based solely on visible observation of morphologic similarities, such as the fact that all birds have wings, even those that do not fly.

Today, there is debate over whether or not all organisms descended from a common ancestor, or a 'last universal ancestor' (LUA), also called the 'last universal common ancestor' (LUCA). The universality of genetic coding suggests common ancestry. For example, every living cell makes use of nucleic acids as its genetic material, and uses the same twenty amino acids as the building blocks for proteins, although exceptions to the basic twenty amino acids have been found. However, throughout history groupings based on appearance or function of species have sometimes been polyphyletic due to convergent evolution.

The 'last universal ancestor' (LUA), or 'last universal common ancestor' (LUCA), is the name given to the hypothetical single cellular organism or single cell that gave rise to all life on Earth 3.5 to 3.8 billion years ago ; however, this hypothesis has since been refuted on many grounds. For example, it was once thought that the genetic code was universal (see: universal genetic code), but many variations have been discovered including various alternative mitochondrial codes. Back in the early 1970s, evolutionary biologists thought that a given piece of DNA specified the same protein subunit in every living thing, and that the genetic code was thus universal. This was interpreted as evidence that every organism had inherited its genetic code from a single common ancestor, aka, an LUCA. In 1979, however, exceptions to the code were found in mitochondria, the tiny energy factories inside cells. Researchers studying human mitochondrial genes discovered that they used an alternative code, and many slight variants have been discovered since, including various alternative mitochondrial codes, as well as small variants such as *Mycoplasma* translating the codon UGA as tryptophan. Biologists subsequently found exceptions in bacteria and in the nuclei of algae and single-celled animals. For example, certain proteins may use alternative initiation (start) codons not normally used by that species. In certain proteins, non-standard amino acids are substituted for standard stop codons, depending upon associated signal sequences in the messenger RNA: UGA can code for selenocysteine and UAG can code for pyrrolysine. Selenocysteine is now viewed as the 21st amino acid, and pyrrolysine is viewed as the 22nd. A detailed description of variations in the genetic code can be found at the NCBI web site.

It is now clear that the genetic code is not the same in all living things and this provides credence that all living things did not evolve on a firmly rooted tree of life from a single LUCA. Further support that there is no LUCA has been provided over the years by horizontal/lateral gene transfer in both prokaryote and eukaryote single cell organisms. This is why phylogenetic trees cannot be rooted; why almost all phylogenetic trees have different branching structures, particularly near the base of the tree; and why many organisms have been found with codons and sections of their DNA sequence that are sometimes unrelated to other species.

Information about the early development of life includes input from many different fields, including geology and planetary science. These sciences provide information about the history of the Earth and the changes produced by life. However, a great deal of information about the early Earth has been destroyed by geological processes over the course of time.

The chemical evolution from self-catalytic chemical reactions to life (see Origin of life) is not a part of biological evolution, but it is unclear at which point such increasingly complex sets of reactions became what we would consider, today, to be living organisms.

Not much is known about the earliest developments in life. However, all existing organisms share certain traits, including cellular structure and genetic code. Most scientists interpret this to mean all existing organisms share a common ancestor, which had already developed the most fundamental cellular processes, but there is no scientific consensus on the relationship of the three domains of life (Archaea, Bacteria, Eukaryota) or the origin of life. Attempts to shed light on the earliest history of life generally focus on the behaviour of macromolecules, particularly RNA, and the behaviour of complex systems.

The emergence of oxygenic photosynthesis (around 3 billion years ago) and the subsequent emergence of an oxygen-rich, non-reducing atmosphere can be traced through the formation of banded iron deposits, and later red beds of iron oxides. This was a necessary prerequisite for the development of aerobic cellular respiration, believed to have emerged around 2 billion years ago.

In the last billion years, simple multicellular plants and animals began to appear in the oceans. Soon after the emergence of the first animals, the Cambrian explosion (a period of unrivaled and remarkable, but brief, organismal diversity documented in the fossils found at the Burgess Shale) saw the creation of all the major body plans, or phyla, of modern animals. This event is now believed to have been triggered by the development of the Hox genes. About 500 million years ago, plants and fungi colonized the land, and were soon followed by arthropods and other animals, leading to the development of today's land ecosystems.

The evolutionary process may be exceedingly slow. Fossil evidence indicates that the diversity and complexity of modern life has developed over much of the history of the earth. Geological evidence indicates that the Earth is approximately 4.6 billion years old. Studies on guppies by David Reznick at the University of California, Riverside, however, have shown that the rate of evolution through natural selection can proceed 10 thousand to 10 million times faster than what is indicated in the fossil record. Such comparative studies however are invariably biased by disparities in the time scales over which evolutionary change is measured in the laboratory, field experiments, and the fossil record.

Horizontal Gene Transfer and the History of Life

The ancestry of living organisms has traditionally been reconstructed from morphology, but is increasingly supplemented with phylogenetics — the reconstruction of phylogenies by the comparison of genetic (DNA) sequence.

"Sequence comparisons suggest recent horizontal transfer of many genes among diverse species including across the boundaries of phylogenetic 'domains'. Thus determining the phylogenetic history of a species can not be done conclusively by determining evolutionary trees for single genes." Biologist Gogarten suggests "the original metaphor of a tree no longer fits the data from recent genome research", therefore "biologists [should] use the metaphor of a mosaic to describe the different histories combined in individual genomes and use [the] metaphor of a net to visualize the rich exchange and cooperative effects of HGT among microbes".

Future of Life (Cloning and Synthetic Organisms)

In modern terms, the category of organism cloning refers to the procedure of creating a new multicellular organism, genetically identical to another. However, cloning also has the potential of creating entirely new species of organisms. Organism cloning is the subject of much ethical debate.

The J. Craig Venter Institute has recently assembled a synthetic yeast genome, *Mycoplasma genitalium*, by recombination of 25 overlapping DNA fragments in a single step. "The use of yeast recombination greatly simplifies the assembly of large DNA molecules from both synthetic and natural fragments." Other companies, such as Synthetic Genomics, have already been formed to take advantage of the many commercial uses of custom designed genomes.

CHAPTER 13

Reproduction

Reproduction is the biological process by which new 'offspring' individual organisms are produced from their 'parents'. Reproduction is a fundamental feature of all known life; each individual organism exists as the result of reproduction. The known methods of reproduction are broadly grouped into two main types: sexual and asexual.

In asexual reproduction, an individual can reproduce without involvement with another individual of that species. The division of a bacterial cell into two daughter cells is an example of asexual reproduction. Asexual reproduction is not, however, limited to single-celled organisms. Most plants have the ability to reproduce asexually.

Sexual reproduction typically requires the involvement of two individuals or gametes, one each from opposite type of sex.

Asexual reproduction is the process by which an organism creates a genetically similar or identical copy of itself without a contribution of genetic material from another individual. Bacteria divide asexually via binary fission; viruses take control of host cells to produce more viruses; Hydras (invertebrates of the order *Hydroidea*) and yeasts are able to reproduce by budding. These organisms often do not possess different sexes, and they are capable of 'splitting' themselves into two or more individuals. On the other hand, some of these species that are capable of reproducing asexually, like hydra, yeast (See Mating of yeasts] and jellyfish, may also reproduce sexually. For instance, most plants are capable of vegetative reproduction—reproduction without seeds or spores—but can also reproduce sexually. Likewise, bacteria may exchange genetic information by conjugation. Other ways of asexual reproduction include parthenogenesis, fragmentation and spore formation that involves only mitosis. Parthenogenesis is the growth and development of embryo or seed without fertilization by a male. Parthenogenesis occurs naturally in some species, including lower plants (where it is called apomixis), invertebrates (e.g. water fleas, aphids, some bees and parasitic wasps), and vertebrates (e.g. some reptiles, fish, and, very rarely, birds and sharks). It is sometimes also used to describe reproduction modes in hermaphroditic species which can self-fertilize.

Sexual Reproduction

Sexual reproduction is a biological process by which organisms create descendants that have a combination of genetic material contributed from two (usually) different members of the species. (Self-fertilization requires only one organism.) Each of two parent organisms contributes half of the offspring's genetic makeup by creating haploid gametes. Most organisms form two different types of gametes. In these *anisogamous* species, the two sexes are referred to as male (producing sperm or microspores) and female (producing ova or megaspores). In *isogamous species*, the gametes are similar or identical in form (isogametes), but may have separable properties and then may be given other different names. For example, in the green alga, *Chlamydomonas reinhardtii*, there are so-called 'plus' and 'minus' gametes. A few types of organisms, such as ciliates, *Paramecium aurelia*, have more than two types of 'sex', called syngens.

Most animals (including humans) and plants reproduce sexually. Sexually reproducing organisms have different sets of genes for every trait (called alleles). Offspring inherit one allele for each trait from each parent, thereby ensuring that offspring have a combination of the parents' genes. Diploid having two copies of every gene within an organism, it is believed that "the masking of deleterious alleles favors the evolution of a dominant diploid phase in organisms that alternate between haploid and diploid phases" where recombination occurs freely.

Bryophyte reproduces sexually but its commonly seen life forms are all haploid, which produce gametes. The zygotes of the gametes develop into sporangium, which produces haploid spores. The diploid stage is relatively short compared with that of haploid stage, i.e. *haploid dominance*. The advantage of diploid, e.g. heterosis, only takes place in diploid life stage. Bryophyte still maintains the sexual reproduction during its evolution despite the fact that the haploid stage does not benefit from heterosis at all. This may be an example that the sexual reproduction has a bigger advantage by itself, since it allows gene shuffling (hybrid or recombination between multiple loci) among different members of the species, that permits natural selection of the fit over these new hybrids or recombinants that are haploid forms.

Allogamy

Allogamy is a term used in the field of biological reproduction describing the fertilization of an ovum from one individual with the spermatozoa of another.

Autogamy

Self-fertilization (also known as autogamy) occurs in hermaphroditic organisms where the two gametes fused in fertilization come from the same individual. They are bound and all the cells merge to form one new gamete.

Mitosis and Meiosis

Mitosis and meiosis are an integral part of cell division. Mitosis occurs in somatic cells, while meiosis occurs in gametes.

Mitosis The resultant number of cells in mitosis is twice the number of original cells. The number of chromosomes in the daughter cells is the same as that of the parent cell.

Meiosis The resultant number of cells is four times the number of original cells. This results in cells with half the number of chromosomes present in the parent cell. A diploid cell duplicates itself, then undergoes two divisions (tetraploid to diploid to haploid), in the process forming four haploid cells. This process occurs in two phases, meiosis I and meiosis II.

Same-sex Reproduction

In recent decades, developmental biologists have been researching and developing techniques to facilitate same-sex reproduction. The obvious approaches, subject to a growing amount of activity, are female sperm and male eggs, with female sperm closer to being a reality for humans, given that Japanese scientists have already created female sperm for chickens. In 2004, by altering the function of a few genes involved with imprinting, other Japanese scientists combined two mouse eggs to produce daughter mice.

Reproductive Strategies

There are a wide range of reproductive strategies employed by different species. Some animals, such as the human and Northern Gannet, do not reach sexual maturity for many years after birth and even then produce few offspring. Others reproduce quickly; but, under normal circumstances, most offspring do not survive to adulthood. For example, a rabbit (mature after 8 months) can produce 10-30 offspring per year, and a fruit fly (mature after 10-14 days) can produce up to 900 offspring per year. These two main strategies are known as *K*-selection (few offspring) and *r*-selection (many offspring). Which strategy is favoured by evolution depends on a variety of circumstances. Animals with few offspring can devote more resources to the nurturing and protection of each individual offspring, thus reducing the need for many offspring. On the other hand, animals with many offspring may devote fewer resources to each individual offspring; for these types of animals it is common for many offspring to die soon after birth, but enough individuals typically survive to maintain the population.

Other Types of Reproductive Strategies

Polycyclic animals reproduce intermittently throughout their lives.

Semelparous organisms reproduce only once in their lifetime, such as annual plants (including all grain crops), and certain species of salmon, spiders, bamboos and centru plants. Often, they die shortly after reproduction. This is often associated with *r*-strategists.

Iteroparous organisms produce offspring in successive (e.g. annual or seasonal) cycles, such as perennial plants. Iteroparous animals survive over multiple seasons (or periodic condition changes). This is more associated with *K*-strategists.

Asexual *vs.* Sexual Reproduction

Organisms that reproduce through asexual reproduction tend to grow in number exponentially. However, because they rely on mutation for variations in their DNA, all members of the species have similar vulnerabilities. Organisms that reproduce sexually yield a smaller number of offspring, but the large amount of variation in their genes makes them less susceptible to disease.

Many organisms can reproduce sexually as well as asexually. Aphids, slime molds, sea anemones, some species of starfish (by fragmentation), and many plants are examples. When environmental factors are favourable, asexual reproduction is employed to exploit suitable conditions for survival such as an abundant food supply, adequate shelter, favourable climate, disease, optimum pH or a proper mix of other lifestyle requirements. Populations of these organisms increase exponentially via asexual reproductive strategies to take full advantage of the rich supply resources.

When food sources have been depleted, the climate becomes hostile, or individual survival is jeopardized by some other adverse change in living conditions, these organisms switch to sexual forms of reproduction. Sexual reproduction ensures a mixing of the gene pool of the species. The variations found in offspring of sexual reproduction allow some individuals to be better suited for survival and provide a mechanism for selective adaptation to occur. In addition, sexual reproduction usually results in the formation of a life stage that is able to endure the conditions that threaten the offspring of an asexual parent. Thus, seeds, spores, eggs, pupae, cysts or other "over-wintering" stages of sexual reproduction ensure the survival during unfavorable times and the organism can 'wait out' adverse situations until a swing back to suitability occurs.

Life without Reproduction

The existence of life without reproduction is the subject of some speculation. The biological study of how the origin of life led from non-reproducing elements to reproducing organisms is called abiogenesis. Whether or not there were several independent abiogenetic events, biologists believe that the last universal ancestor to all present life on earth lived about 3.5 billion years ago.

Today, some scientists have speculated about the possibility of creating life non-reproductively in the laboratory. Several scientists have succeeded in producing simple viruses from entirely non-living materials. The virus is often regarded as not alive. Being nothing more than a bit of RNA or DNA in a protein capsule, they have no metabolism and can only replicate with the assistance of a hijacked cell's metabolic machinery.

The production of a truly living organism (*e.g.*, a simple bacterium) with no ancestors would be a much more complex task, but may well be possible according to current biological knowledge. A synthetic genome has been transferred into an existing bacterium where it replaced the native DNA, resulting in the artificial production of a new M. mycoides organism.

Lottery Principle

Sexual reproduction has many drawbacks, since it requires far more energy than asexual reproduction and diverts the organisms from other pursuits, and there is some argument about why so many species use it.

George C. Williams used lottery tickets as an analogy in one explanation for the widespread use of sexual reproduction . He argued that asexual reproduction, which produces little or no genetic variety in offspring, was like buying many tickets that all have the same number, limiting the chance of 'winning' — that is, producing surviving offspring. Sexual reproduction, he argued, was like purchasing fewer tickets but with a greater variety of numbers and therefore a greater chance of success.

The point of this analogy is that since asexual reproduction does not produce genetic variations, there is little ability to quickly adapt to a changing environment. The lottery principle is less accepted these days because of evidence that asexual reproduction is more prevalent in unstable environments, the opposite of what it predicts.

CHAPTER 14

Null Hypothesis

The practice of science involves formulating and testing *hypothesis*, assertions that are falsifiable using a test of observed data. The null hypothesis typically proposes a general or default position, such as that there is no relationship between two measured phenomena, or that a potential treatment has no effect. The term was originally coined by English geneticist and statistician Ronald Fisher. It is typically paired with a second hypothesis, the alternative hypothesis, which asserts a particular relationship between the phenomena. Jerzy Neyman and Egon Pearson formalized the notion of the alternative. The alternative need not be the logical negation of the null hypothesis and is the predicted hypothesis you would get from the experiment. The use of alternative hypothesis was not part of Fisher's formulation, but became standard.

Hypothesis testing works by collecting data and measuring how probable the data are, assuming the null hypothesis is true. If the data are very improbable (usually defined as observed less than 5 per cent of the time), then the experimenter concludes that the null hypothesis is false. If the data do not contradict the null hypothesis, then no conclusion is made. In this case, the null hypothesis could be true or false; the data give insufficient evidence to make any conclusion.

For instance, a certain drug may reduce the chance of having a heart attack. Possible null hypothesis are "this drug does not reduce the chances of having a heart attack" and "this drug has no effect on the chances of having a heart attack". The test of the hypothesis consists of administering the drug to half of the people in a study group as a controlled experiment. If the data show a statistically significant change in the people receiving the drug, the null hypothesis is rejected.

The choice of null hypothesis is critical. Consider the question of whether a tossed coin is fair (i.e. that on average it lands heads up 50% of the time). A potential null hypothesis is "this coin is not biased towards heads". The experiment is to repeatedly toss the coin. A possible result of 5 tosses is 5 heads. Under this null hypothesis, the data are considered unlikely (with a fair coin, the probability of this is 3%). The data refute the null hypothesis: the coin is biased.

Alternatively, the null hypothesis, 'this coin is fair' allows runs of tails as well as heads, increasing the probability of 5 of a kind to 6 per cent, which is no longer statistically significant, preserving the null hypothesis.

This example illustrates one hazard of hypothesis testing: evaluating a large number of true null hypothesis against a single dataset is likely to spuriously reject some of them because of the inevitable noise in the data. However, formulating the null hypothesis before collecting data, rejects a true null hypothesis only a small per cent of the time.

In scientific and medical research, null hypothesis play a major role in testing the significance of differences in treatment and control groups. This use, while widespread, offers several grounds for criticism, including straw man, Bayesian criticism and publication bias.

The typical null hypothesis at the outset of the experiment is that no difference exists between the control and experimental groups (for the variable being compared). Other possibilities include:

- that values in samples from a given population can be modeled using a certain family of statistical distributions.
- that the variability of data in different groups is the same, although they may be centered around different values.

Directionality

Quite often statements of null hypothesis appear not to have a 'directionality', namely, that values are identical. However, null hypothesis can and do have 'direction'—in many instances statistical theory allows the formulation of the test procedure to be simplified, thus the test is equivalent to testing for an exact identity. For instance, when formulating a one-tailed alternative hypothesis, *application of Drug A will lead to increased growth in patients*, then the true null hypothesis is the opposite of the alternative hypothesis i.e. *application of Drug A will not lead to increased growth in patients*. The effective null hypothesis will be *application of Drug A will have no effect on growth in patients*.

In order to understand why the effective null hypothesis is valid, it is instructive to consider the above hypothesis. The alternative predicts that exposed patients experience increased growth compared to the control group. That is:

$H_1 : \mu_{drug} > \mu_{control}$

where:

μ = the patients' mean growth.

The effective null hypothesis is $H_0 : \mu_{drug} = \mu_{control}$.

The true null hypothesis is.

The reduction occurs because, in order to gauge support for the alternative, classical hypothesis testing requires calculating how often the results would be as or more extreme than the observations. This requires measuring the probability of rejecting the null hypothesis for each possibility it includes and second to ensure that these probabilities are all less than or equal to the test's quoted significance level. For reasonable test procedures the largest such probability occurs on the region boundary H_T, specifically for the cases included in H_0 only. Thus the test procedure can be defined (that is the critical values can be defined) for testing the null hypothesis H_T exactly as if the null hypothesis of interest was the reduced version H_0.

Fisher said, "the null hypothesis must be exact, that is free of vagueness and ambiguity, because it must supply the basis of the 'problem of distribution,' of which the test of significance is the solution", implying a more restrictive domain for H_0. According to this view, the null hypothesis must be numerically exact—it must state that a particular quantity or difference is equal to a particular number. In classical science, it is most typically the statement that there is *no effect* of a particular treatment; in observations, it is typically that there is *no difference* between the value of a particular measured variable and that of a prediction. The majority of null hypothesis in practice do not meet this 'exactness' criterion. For example, consider the usual test that two means are equal where the true values of the variances are unknown—exact values of the variances are not specified.

Most statisticians believe that it is valid to state direction as a part of null hypothesis, or as part of a null hypothesis/alternative hypothesis pair. The logic is quite simple: if the direction is omitted, then if the null hypothesis is not rejected it is quite confusing to interpret the conclusion. For example, consider an H_0 that claims the population mean = 10, with the one-tailed alternative mean > 10. If the sample evidence obtained through x-bar equals -200 and the corresponding t-test statistic equals -50, what is the conclusion? Not enough evidence to reject the null hypothesis? Surely not! But we cannot accept the one-sided alternative in this case. Therefore, to overcome this ambiguity, it is better to include the direction of the effect if the test is one-sided. The statistical theory required to deal with the simple cases dealt with here, and more complicated ones, makes use of the concept of an unbiased test.

Sample Size

Statistical hypothesis testing involves performing the same experiment on multiple subjects. The number of subjects is known as the sample size. The procedure depends on the size. Even if a null hypothesis does not hold for the population, an insufficient sample size may prevent its rejection. Minimum sample size depends on the statistical power of the test, the effect size that the test must reveal and the desired significance level. The significance level is the probability of rejecting the null hypothesis when the null hypothesis holds in the population. The statistical power is the probability of rejecting the null hypothesis when it does not hold in the population (i.e., for a particular effect size).

Hypothesis

A hypothesis is a proposed explanation for an observable phenomenon. The term derives from the Greek, *hypotithenai* meaning 'to put under' or 'to suppose'. For a hypothesis to be put forward as a scientific hypothesis, the scientific method requires that one can test it. Scientists generally base scientific hypothesis on previous observations that cannot satisfactorily be explained with the available scientific theories. Even though the words 'hypothesis' and 'theory' are often used synonymously in common and informal usage, a scientific *hypothesis* is not the same as a scientific *theory*. A working hypothesis is a provisionally accepted hypothesis.

In a related but distinguishable usage, the term hypothesis is used for the antecedent of a proposition; thus in proposition 'If *P*, then *Q*', *P* denotes the hypothesis (or antecedent); *Q* can be called a consequent. *P* is the assumption in a (possibly counterfactual) *What If* question.

The adjective hypothetical, meaning 'having the nature of a hypothesis', or 'being assumed to exist as an immediate consequence of a hypothesis', can refer to any of these meanings of the term 'hypothesis'.

In its ancient usage, hypothesis also refers to a summary of the plot of a classical drama.

In Plato's *Meno* , Socrates dissects virtue with a method used by mathematicians, that of "investigating from a hypothesis." In this sense, 'hypothesis' refers to a clever idea or to a convenient mathematical approach that simplifies cumbersome calculations. Cardinal Bellarmine gave a famous example of this usage in the warning issued to Galileo in the early 17th century: that he must not treat the motion of the Earth as a reality, but merely as a hypothesis.

In common usage in the 21st century, a *hypothesis* refers to a provisional idea whose merit requires evaluation. For proper evaluation, the framer of a hypothesis needs to define specifics in operational terms. A hypothesis requires more work by the researcher in order to either confirm or disprove it. In due course, a confirmed hypothesis may become part of a theory or occasionally may grow to become a theory itself. Normally, scientific hypothesis have the form of a mathematical model. Sometimes, but not always, one can also formulate them as existential statements, stating that some particular instance of the phenomenon under examination has some characteristic and causal explanations, which have the general form of universal statements, stating that every instance of the phenomenon has a particular characteristic.

Any useful hypothesis will enable predictions by reasoning (including deductive reasoning). It might predict the outcome of an experiment in a laboratory setting or the observation of a phenomenon in nature. The prediction may also invoke statistics and only talk about probabilities. Karl Popper, following others, has argued that a hypothesis must be falsifiable, and that one cannot regard a proposition or theory as scientific if it does not admit the possibility of shown false. Other philosophers of science have rejected the criterion of falsifiability or supplemented it with other criteria, such as verifiability (e.g., verificationism) or coherence (e.g., confirmation holism). The scientific method involves experimentation on the basis of hypothesis in order to answer questions and explore observations.

In framing a hypothesis, the investigator must not currently know the outcome of a test or that it remains reasonably under continuing investigation. Only in such cases does the experiment, test or study potentially increase the probability of showing the truth of a hypothesis. If the researcher already knows the outcome, it counts as a 'consequence' — and the researcher should have already considered this while formulating the hypothesis. If one cannot assess the predictions by observation or by experience, the hypothesis classes as not yet useful, and must wait for others who might come afterward to make possible the needed observations. For example, a new technology or theory might make the necessary experiments feasible.

Scientific Hypothesis

People refer to a trial solution to a problem as a hypothesis — often called an 'educated guess' — because it provides a suggested solution based on the evidence. Experimenters may test and reject several hypothesis before solving the problem.

According to Schick and Vaughn, researchers weighing up alternative hypothesis may take into consideration:

- Testability (compare falsifiability as discussed above)
- Simplicity (as in the application of 'Occam's razor', discouraging the postulation of excessive numbers of entities)
- Scope — the apparent application of the hypothesis to multiple cases of phenomena
- Fruitfulness — the prospect that a hypothesis may explain further phenomena in the future
- Conservatism — the degree of 'fit' with existing recognized knowledge-systems

Evaluating Hypothesis

Karl Popper's formulation of hypothetico-deductive method, which he called the method of 'conjectures and refutations', demands falsifiable hypothesis, framed in such a manner that the scientific community can prove them false (usually by observation). According to this view, a hypothesis cannot be "confirmed", because there is always the possibility that a future experiment will show that it is false. Hence, failing to falsify a hypothesis does not prove that hypothesis: it remains provisional. However, a hypothesis that has been rigorously tested and not falsified can form a reasonable basis for action, i.e., we can act as if it were true, until such time as it is falsified. Just because we've never observed rain falling upward, doesn't mean that we never will–however improbable, our theory of gravity may be falsified some day.

Popper's view is not the only view on evaluating hypothesis. For example, some forms of empiricism hold that under a well-crafted, well-controlled experiment, a lack of falsification *does* count as verification, since such an experiment ranges over the full scope of possibilities in the problem domain. Should we ever discover some place where gravity did not function, and rain fell upward, this would not falsify our current theory of gravity (which, on this view, has been verified by innumerable well-formed experiments in the past) — it would rather suggest an expansion of our theory to encompass some new force or previously undiscovered interaction of forces. In other words, our initial theory as it stands is verified but incomplete. This situation illustrates the importance of having well-crafted, well-controlled experiments that range over the full scope of possibilities for applying the theory.

In recent years philosophers of science have tried to integrate the various approaches to evaluating hypothesis, and the scientific method in general, to form a more complete system that integrates the individual concerns of each approach. Notably, Imre Lakatos and Paul Feyerabend, both former students of Popper, have produced novel attempts at such a synthesis.

Hypothesis, Concepts and Measurement

Concepts, as abstract units of meaning, play a key role in the development and testing of hypothesis. Concepts are the basic components of hypothesis. Most formal hypothesis connect concepts by specifying the expected relationships between concepts. For example, a simple relational hypothesis such as 'education increases income' specifies a positive relationship between the concepts 'education' and 'income'. This abstract or conceptual hypothesis cannot be tested. First, it must be operationalized or situated in the real world by rules of interpretation. Consider again the simple hypothesis 'Education increases Income'. To test the hypothesis the abstract meaning of education and income must be derived or operationalized. The concepts should be measured. Education could be measured by 'years of school completed' or 'highest degree completed' etc. Income could be measured by 'hourly rate of pay' or 'yearly salary' etc.

When a set of hypothesis are grouped together they become a type of conceptual framework. When a conceptual framework is complex and incorporates causality or explanation it is generally referred to as a theory. According to noted philosopher of science Carl Gustav Hempel "An adequate empirical interpretation turns a theoretical system into a testable theory: The hypothesis whose constituent terms have been interpreted become capable of test by reference to observable phenomena. Frequently the interpreted hypothesis will be derivative hypothesis of the theory; but their confirmation or disconfirmation by empirical data will then immediately strengthen or weaken also the primitive hypothesis from which they were derived".

Hempel provides a useful metaphor that describes the relationship between a conceptual framework and the framework as it is observed and perhaps tested (interpreted framework). "The whole system floats, as it were, above the plane of observation and is anchored to it by rules of interpretation. These might be viewed as strings which are not part of the network but link certain points of the latter with specific places in the plane of observation. By virtue of those interpretative connections, the network can function as a scientific theory" Hypothesis with concepts anchored in the plane of observation are ready to be tested. In "actual scientific practice the process of framing a theoretical structure and of interpreting it are not always sharply separated, since the intended interpretation usually guides the construction of the theoretician." It is, however, "possible and indeed desirable, for the purposes of logical clarification, to separate the two steps conceptually".

When a possible correlation or similar relation between phenomena is investigated, such as, for example, whether a proposed remedy is effective in treating a disease, that is, at least to some extent and for some patients, the hypothesis that a relation exists cannot be examined the same way one might examine a proposed new law of nature: in such an investigation a few cases in which the tested remedy shows no effect do not falsify the hypothesis. Instead, statistical tests are used to determine how likely it is that the overall effect would be observed if no real relation as hypothesized exists. If that likelihood is sufficiently small (e.g., less than 1%), the existence of a relation may be assumed. Otherwise, any observed effect may as well be due to pure chance.

In statistical hypothesis testing two hypothesis are compared, which are called the null hypothesis and the alternative hypothesis. The null hypothesis is the hypothesis that states that there is no relation between the phenomena whose relation is under investigation, or at least not of the form given by the alternative hypothesis. The alternative hypothesis, as the name suggests, is the alternative to the null hypothesis: it states that there *is* some kind of relation. The alternative hypothesis may take several forms, depending on the nature of the hypothesized relation; in particular, it can be two-sided (for example: there is *some* effect, in a yet unknown direction) or one-sided (the direction of the hypothesized relation, positive or negative, is fixed in advance).

Proper use of statistical testing requires that these hypothesis, and the threshold (such as 1%) at which the null hypothesis is rejected and the alternative hypothesis is accepted, all be determined in advance, before the observations are collected or inspected. If these criteria are determined later, when the data to be tested is already known, the test is invalid.

CHAPTER 15
Demography

Demography is the statistical study of human populations. It can be a very general science that can be applied to any kind of dynamic human population, that is, one that changes over time or space. It encompasses the study of the size, structure and distribution of these populations, and spatial and/or temporal changes in them in response to birth, migration, aging and death.

Demographic analysis can be applied to whole societies or to groups defined by criteria such as education, nationality, religion and ethnicity. Institutionally, demography is usually considered a field of sociology, though there are a number of independent demography departments. Formal demography limits its object of study to the measurement of populations processes, while the more broad field of social demography population studies also analyze the relationships between economic, social, cultural and biological processes influencing a population.

The term demographics is often used erroneously for demography, but refers rather to selected population characteristics as used in government, marketing or opinion research, or the demographic profiles used in such research.

There are two methods of data collection: direct and indirect. Direct data come from vital statistics registries that track all births and deaths as well as certain changes in legal status such as marriage, divorce, and migration (registration of place of residence). In developed countries with good registration systems (such as the United States and much of Europe), registry statistics are the best method for estimating the number of births and deaths.

A census is the other common direct method of collecting demographic data. A census is usually conducted by a national government and attempts to enumerate every person in a country. However, in contrast to vital statistics data, which are typically collected continuously and summarized on an annual basis, censuses typically occur only every 10 years or so, and thus are not usually the best source of data on births and deaths. Analyses are conducted after a census to estimate how much over or undercounting took place.

Censuses do more than just count people. They typically collect information about families or households, as well as about such individual characteristics as age, sex, marital status, literacy/education, employment status and occupation, and geographical location. They may also collect data on migration (or place of birth or of previous residence), language, religion, nationality (or ethnicity or race), and citizenship. In countries in which the vital registration system may be incomplete, the censuses are also used as a direct source of information about fertility and mortality; for example the censuses of the People's Republic of China gather information on births and deaths that occurred in the 18 months immediately preceding the census.

Indirect methods of collecting data are required in countries where full data are not available, such as is the case in much of the developing world. One of these techniques is the sister method, where survey researchers ask women how many of their sisters have died or had children and at what age. With these surveys, researchers can then indirectly estimate birth or death rates for the entire population. Other indirect methods include asking people about siblings, parents, and children.

There are a variety of demographic methods for modeling population processes. They include models of mortality (including the life table, Gompertz models, hazards models, Cox proportional hazards models, multiple decrement life tables, Brass relational logits), fertility (Hernes model, Coale-Trussell models, parity progression ratios), marriage (Singulate Mean at Marriage, Page model), disability (Sullivan's method, multistate life tables), population projections (Lee Carter, the Leslie Matrix), and population momentum (Keyfitz).

- The crude *birth rate,* the annual number of live births per 1,000 people.
- The general *fertility rate,* the annual number of live births per 1,000 women of childbearing age (often taken to be from 15 to 49 years old, but sometimes from 15 to 44).
- age-specific fertility rates, the annual number of live births per 1,000 women in particular age groups (usually age 15-19, 20-24 etc.)
- The crude *death rate,* the annual number of deaths per 1,000 people.
- The *infant mortality rate,* the annual number of deaths of children less than 1 year old per 1,000 live births.

- The expectation of life (or life expectancy), the number of years which an individual at a given age could expect to live at present mortality levels.
- The *total fertility rate*, the number of live births per woman completing her reproductive life, if her childbearing at each age reflected current age-specific fertility rates.
- The replacement level fertility, the average number of children a woman must have in order to replace herself with a daughter in the next generation. For example the replacement level fertility in the US is 2.11. This means that 100 women will bear 211 children, 103 of which will be females. About 3 per cent of the alive female infants are expected to decease before they bear children, thus producing 100 women in the next generation.
- The *gross reproduction rate*, the number of daughters who would be born to a woman completing her reproductive life at current age-specific fertility rates.
- The net reproduction ratio is the expected number of daughters, per newborn prospective mother, who may or may not survive to and through the ages of childbearing.
- A stable population, one that has had constant crude birth and death rates for such long time that the percentage of people in every age class remains constant, or equivalently, the population pyramid has an unchanging structure.
- A stationary population, one that is both stable and unchanging in size (the difference between crude birth rate and crude death rate is zero).

A stable population does not necessarily remain fixed in size, it can be expanding or shrinking.

Note that the crude death rate as defined above and applied to a whole population can give a misleading impression. For example, the number of deaths per 1,000 people can be higher for developed nations than in less-developed countries, despite standards of health being better in developed countries. This is because developed countries have proportionally more older people, who are more likely to die in a given year, so that the overall mortality rate can be higher even if the mortality rate at any given age is lower. A more complete picture of mortality is given by a life table which summarises mortality separately at each age. A life table is necessary to give a good estimate of life expectancy.

The fertility rates can also give a misleading impression that a population is growing faster than it in fact is, because measurement of fertility rates only involves the reproductive rate of women, and does not adjust for the sex ratio. For example, if a population has a total fertility rate of 4.0 but the sex ratio is 66/34 (twice as many men as women), this population is actually growing at a slower natural increase rate than would a population having a fertility rate of 3.0 and a sex ratio of 50/50. This distortion is greatest in India and Myanmar, and is present in China as well.

Basic Equation

Suppose that a country (or other entity) contains $Population_t$ persons at time t. What is the size of the population at time $t + 1$?

$$Population_{t+1} = Population_t + Naturalincrease_t + Netmigration_t$$

Natural increase from time t to $t + 1$:

$$Naturalincrease_t = Births_t - Deaths_t$$

Net migration from time t to $t + 1$:

$$Netmigration_t = Immigration_t - Emigration_t$$

This basic equation can also be applied to subpopulations. For example, the population size of ethnic groups or nationalities within a given society or country is subject to the same sources of change. However, when dealing with ethnic groups, 'net migration' might have to be subdivided into physical migration and ethnic reidentification (assimilation). Individuals who change their ethnic self-labels or whose ethnic classification in government statistics changes over time may be thought of as migrating or moving from one population subcategory to another.

More generally, while the basic demographic equation holds true by definition, in practice the recording and counting of events (births, deaths, immigration, emigration) and the enumeration of the total population size are subject to error. So allowance needs to be made for error in the underlying statistics when any accounting of population size or change is made.

Demographic thoughts can be traced back to antiquity, and are present in many civilisations and cultures, like Ancient Greece, Rome, India and China. In ancient Greece,this can be found in the writings of Herodotus, Thucidides, Hippocrates, Epicurus, Protagoras, Polus, Plato and Aristotle. In Rome,writers and philosophers like Cicero, Seneca, Pliny the elder, Marcus Aurelius, Epictetus, Cato and Collumella alse expressed important ideas on this ground.

In the Middle ages, Christian thinkers devoted much time in refuting the roman ideas on demography. Important contributors to the field were William of Conches, Bartholomew of Lucca, William of Auvergne, William of Pagula, and Ibn Khaldun.

The *Natural and Political Observations . . . upon the Bills of Mortality* (1662) of John Graunt contains a primitive form of life table. Mathematicians, such as Edmond Halley, developed the life table as the basis for life insurance mathematics. Richard Price was credited with the first textbook on life contingencies published in 1771, followed later by Augustus de Morgan, 'On the Application of Probabilities to Life Contingencies' (1838).

At the end of the 18th century, Thomas Malthus concluded that, if unchecked, populations would be subject to exponential growth. He feared that population growth would tend to outstrip growth in food production, leading to ever-increasing famine and poverty . He is seen as the intellectual father of ideas of overpopulation and the limits to growth. Later, more sophisticated and realistic models were presented by Benjamin Gompertz and Verhulst.

The period 1860-1910 can be characterized as a period of transition wherein demography emerged from statistics as a separate field of interest. This period included a panoply of international 'great demographers' like Adolphe Quételet (1796-1874), William Farr (1807-1883), Louis-Adolphe Bertillon (1821-1883) and his son Jacques (1851-1922), Joseph Körösi (1844-1906), Anders Nicolas Kaier (1838-1919), Richard Böckh (1824-1907), Wilhelm Lexis (1837-1914) and Luigi Bodio (1840-1920) contributed to the development of demography and to the toolkit of methods and techniques of demographic analysis.

Contrary to Malthus' predictions and in line with his thoughts on moral restraint, natural population growth in most developed countries has diminished to close to zero, without being held in check by famine or lack of resources, as people in developed nations have shown a tendency to have fewer children. The fall in population growth has occurred despite large rises in life expectancy in these countries. This pattern of population growth, with slow (or no) growth in pre-industrial societies, followed by fast growth as the society develops and industrializes, followed by slow growth again as it becomes more affluent, is known as the demographic transition.

Similar trends are now becoming visible in ever more developing countries, so that far from spiraling out of control, world population growth is expected to slow markedly in this century, coming to an eventual standstill or even declining. The change is likely to be accompanied by major shifts in the proportion of world population in particular regions. The United Nations Population Division expects the absolute number of infants and toddlers in the world to begin to fall by 2015, and the number of children under 15 by 2025.

The figure in this section shows the latest (2004) UN projections of world population out to the year 2150 (red = high, orange = medium, green = low). The UN 'medium' projection shows world population reaching an approximate equilibrium at 9 billion by 2075. Working independently, demographers at the International Institute for Applied Systems Analysis in Austria expect world population to peak at 9 billion by 2070. Throughout the 21st century, the average age of the population is likely to continue to rise.

Populations can change through three processes: fertility, mortality, and migration. Fertility involves the number of children that women have and is to be contrasted with fecundity (a woman's childbearing potential). Mortality is the study of the causes, consequences, and measurement of processes affecting death to members of the population. Demographers most commonly study mortality using the Life Table, a statistical device which provides information about the mortality conditions (most notably the life expectancy) in the population.

Migration refers to the movement of persons from an origin place to a destination place across some pre-defined, political boundary. Migration researchers do not designate movements 'migrations' unless they are somewhat permanent. Thus demographers do not consider tourists and travelers to be migrating. While demographers who study migration typically do so through census data on place of residence, indirect sources of data including tax forms and labor force surveys are also important.

Demography is today widely taught in many universities across the world, attracting students with initial training in social sciences, statistics or health studies. Being at the crossroads of several disciplines such as sociology, economics, epidemiology, geography, anthropology and history, demography offers tools to approach a large range of population issues by combining a more technical quantitative approach that represents the core of the discipline with many other methods borrowed from social or other sciences. Demographic research is conducted in universities, in research institutes as well as in statistical departments and in several international agencies. Population institutions are part of the Cicred (International Committee for Coordination of Demographic Research) network while most individual scientists engaged in demographic research are members of the International Union for the Scientific Study of Population or, in the United States, the Population Association of America.

Ecoregion

An ecoregion (ecological region), sometimes called a bioregion, is an ecologically and geographically defined area that is smaller than an ecozone and larger than an ecosystem. Ecoregions cover relatively large areas of land or water, and contain characteristic, geographically distinct assemblages of natural communities and species. The biodiversity of flora, fauna and ecosystems that characterise an ecoregion tends to be distinct from that of other ecoregions.

An ecoregion is a "recurring pattern of ecosystems associated with characteristic combinations of soil and landform that characterise that region" Omernik (2004), elaborates on this by defining ecoregions as: "areas within which there is spatial coincidence in characteristics of geographical phenomena associated with differences in the quality, health, and integrity of ecosystems" "Characteristics of geographical phenomena" may include geology, physiography, vegetation, climate, hydrology, terrestrial and aquatic fauna, and soils, and may or may not include the impacts of human activity (e.g. land use patterns, vegetation changes). There is significant, but not absolute, spatial correlation among these characteristics, making the delineation of ecoregions an imperfect science. Another complication is that environmental conditions across an ecoregion boundary may change very gradually, e.g. the prairie-forest transition in the midwestern United States, making it difficult to identify an exact dividing boundary. Such transition zones are called ecotones.

Ecoregions can be categorized using an algorithmic approach or a holistic, 'weight-of-evidence' approach where the importance of various factors may vary. An example of the algorithmic approach is Robert Bailey's work for the U.S. Forest Service, which uses a hierarchical classification that first divides land areas into very large regions based on climatic factors, and subdivides these regions, based first on dominant potential vegetation, and then by geomorphology and soil characteristics. The weight-of-evidence approach is exemplified by James Omernik's work for the United States Environmental Protection Agency, subsequently adopted (with modification) for North America by the Commission for Environmental Cooperation.

The intended purpose of ecoregion delineation may affect the method used. For example, the WWF ecoregions were developed to aid in biodiversity conservation planning, and place a greater emphasis than the Omernik or Bailey systems on floral and faunal differences between regions. The WWF classification defines an ecoregion as:

A large area of land or water that contains a geographically distinct assemblage of natural communities that:

(a) share a large majority of their species and ecological dynamics;

(b) share similar environmental conditions, and;

(c) interact ecologically in ways that are critical for their long-term persistence.

According to WWF, the boundaries of an ecoregion approximate the original extent of the natural communities prior to any major recent disruptions or changes. WWF has identified 867 terrestrial ecoregions, and approximately 450 freshwater ecoregions across the Earth.

The use of the term ecoregion is an outgrowth of a surge of interest in ecosystems and their functioning. In particular, there is awareness of issues relating to spatial scale in the study and management of landscapes. It is widely recognized that interlinked ecosystems combine to form a whole that is 'greater than the sum of its parts'. There are many attempts to respond to ecosystems in an integrated way to achieve 'multi-functional' landscapes, and various interest groups from agricultural researchers to conservationists are using the "ecoregion" as a unit of analysis.

The 'Global 200' is the list of ecoregions identified by WWF as priorities for conservation.

Ecologically-based movements like bioregionalism maintain that ecoregions, rather than arbitrarily-defined political boundaries, provide a better foundation for the formation and governance of human communities, and have proposed ecoregions and watersheds as the basis for bioregional democracy initiatives.

Terrestrial ecoregions are land ecoregions, as distinct from freshwater and marine ecoregions. In this context, *terrestrial* is used to mean "of land" (soil and rock), rather than the more general sense 'of Earth' (which includes land and oceans).

World Wildlife Fund (WWF) ecologists currently divide the land surface of the Earth into 8 major ecozones containing 867 smaller terrestrial ecoregions (see list). The WWF effort is a synthesis of many previous efforts to define and classify ecoregions. Many consider this classification to be quite decisive, and some propose these as stable borders for bioregional democracy initiatives.

The eight terrestrial ecozones follow the major floral and faunal boundaries, identified by botanists and zoologists, that separate the world's major plant and animal communities. Ecozone boundaries generally follow continental boundaries, or major barriers to plant and animal distribution, like the Himalayas and the Sahara. The boundaries of ecoregions are often not as decisive or well recognized, and are subject to greater disagreement.

Ecoregions are classified by biome type, which are the major global plant communities determined by rainfall and climate. Forests, grasslands (including savanna and shrubland), and deserts (including xeric shrublands) are distinguished by climate (tropical and subtropical *vs.* temperate and boreal climates) and, for forests, by whether the trees are predominantly conifers (gymnosperms), or whether they are predominantly broadleaf (Angiosperms) and mixed (broadleaf and conifer). Biome types like Mediterranean forests, woodlands, and scrub; tundra; and mangroves host very distinct ecological communities, and are recognized as distinct biome types as well.

Marine ecoregions are: "Areas of relatively homogeneous species composition, clearly distinct from adjacent systems. . . . In ecological terms, these are strongly cohesive units, sufficiently large to encompass ecological or life history processes for most sedentary species." They have been defined by The Nature Conservancy (TNC) and World Wildlife Fund (WWF) to aid in conservation activities for marine ecosystems. Forty-three priority marine ecoregions were delineated as part of WWF's Global 200 efforts. The scheme used to designate and classify marine ecoregions is analogous to that used for terrestrial ecoregions. Major habitat types are identified: polar, temperate shelves and seas, temperate upwelling, tropical upwelling, tropical coral, pelagic (trades and westerlies), abyssal, and hadal (ocean trench). These correspond to the terrestrial biomes.

The Global 200 classification of marine ecoregions is not developed to the same level of detail and comprehensiveness as that of the terrestrial ecoregions; only the priority conservation areas are listed.

In 2007, TNC and WWF refined and expanded this scheme to provide a system of comprehensive near shore (to 200 meters depth) Marine Ecoregions of the World (MEOW). The 232 individual marine ecoregions are grouped into 62 marine provinces, which in turn group into 12 marine realms, which represent the broad latitudinal divisions of polar, temperate, and tropical seas, with subdivisions based on ocean basins (except for the southern hemisphere temperate oceans, which are based on continents).

Major biogeographic realms, analogous to the eight terrestrial ecozones, represent large regions of the ocean basins: Arctic, Temperate Northern Atlantic, Temperate Northern Pacific, Tropical Atlantic, Western Indo-Pacific, Central Indo-Pacific, Eastern Indo-Pacific, Tropical Eastern Pacific, Temperate South America, Temperate Southern Africa, Temperate Australasia, Southern Ocean.

A similar system of identifying areas of the oceans for conservation purposes is the system of large marine ecosystems (LMEs), developed by the US National Oceanic and Atmospheric Administration (NOAA).

A freshwater ecoregion is a large area encompassing one or more freshwater systems that contains a distinct assemblage of natural freshwater communities and species. The freshwater species, dynamics, and environmental conditions within a given ecoregion are more similar to each other than to those of surrounding ecoregions and together form a conservation unit. Freshwater systems include rivers, streams, lakes, and wetlands. Freshwater ecoregions are distinct from terrestrial ecoregions, which identify biotic communities of the land, and marine ecoregions, which are biotic communities of the oceans.

A new map of Freshwater Ecoregions of the World, released in 2008, has 426 ecoregions covering virtually the entire non-marine surface of the earth.

World Wildlife Fund (WWF) identifies twelve major habitat types of freshwater ecoregions: Large lakes, large river deltas, polar freshwaters, montane freshwaters, temperate coastal rivers, temperate floodplain rivers and wetlands, temperate upland rivers, tropical and subtropical coastal rivers, tropical and subtropical floodplain rivers and wetlands, tropical and subtropical upland rivers, xeric freshwaters and endorheic basins, and oceanic islands. The freshwater major habitat types reflect groupings of ecoregions with similar biological, chemical, and physical characteristics and are roughly equivalent to biomes for terrestrial systems.

The Global 200, a set of ecoregions identified by WWF whose conservation would achieve the goal of saving a broad diversity of the Earth's ecosystems, includes a number of areas highlighted for their freshwater biodiversity values. The Global 200 preceded Freshwater Ecoregions of the World and incorporated information from regional freshwater ecoregional assessments that had been completed at that time.

Biome

Biomes are climatically and geographically defined as similar climatic conditions on the Earth, such as communities of plants, animals, and soil organisms, and are often referred to as ecosystems. Some parts of the earth have more or less the same kind of abiotic and biotic factors spread over a large area creating a typical ecosystem over that area. Such major ecosystems are termed as biomes. Biomes are defined by factors such as plant structures (such as trees, shrubs, and grasses), leaf types (such as broadleaf and needleleaf), plant spacing (forest, woodland, savanna), and climate. Unlike ecozones, biomes are not defined by genetic, taxonomic, or historical similarities. Biomes are often identified with particular patterns of ecological succession and climax vegetation (quasi-equilibrium state of the local ecosystem). An ecosystem has many biotopes and a biome is a major habitat type. A major habitat type, however, is a compromise, as it has an intrinsic inhomogeneity.

The biodiversity characteristic of each biome, especially the diversity of fauna and subdominant plant forms, is a function of abiotic factors and the biomass productivity of the dominant vegetation. In terrestrial biomes, species diversity tends to correlate positively with net primary productivity, moisture availability, and temperature.

Ecoregions are grouped into both biomes and ecozones.

A fundamental classification of biomes is:

- Terrestrial (land) biomes
- Aquatic biomes (including Freshwater biomes and Marine biomes)

Biomes are often known in English by local names. For example, a temperate grassland or shrubland biome is known commonly as *steppe* in central Asia, *prairie* in North America, and *pampas* in South America. Tropical grasslands are known as *savanna* in Australia, whereas in Southern Africa it is known as *veldt* (from Afrikaans).

Sometimes an entire biome may be targeted for protection, especially under an individual nation's Biodiversity Action Plan.

Climate is a major factor determining the distribution of terrestrial biomes. Among the important climatic factors are:

- *Latitude:* Arctic, boreal, temperate, subtropical, tropical.
- *Humidity:* humid, semi-humid, semi-arid, and arid.
- *Seasonal variation:* Rainfall may be distributed evenly throughout the year or be marked by seasonal variations.

- *Dry summer, wet winter:* Most regions of the earth receive most of their rainfall during the summer months; Mediterranean climate regions receive their rainfall during the winter months.
- *Elevation:* Increasing elevation causes a distribution of habitat types similar to that of increasing latitude.

The most widely used systems of classifying biomes correspond to latitude (or temperature zoning) and humidity. Biodiversity generally increases away from the poles towards the equator and increases with humidity.

Biome classification schemes seek to define biomes using climatic measurements. Particularly in the 1970s and 1980s there was a significant push to understand the relationships between these measurements and properties of ecosystem energetics because such discoveries would enable the prediction of rates of energy capture and transfer among components within ecosystems. Such a study was conducted by Sims et al. (1978) on North American grasslands. The study found a positive logistic correlation between evapotranspiration in mm/yr and above ground net primary production in g/m^2/yr. More general results from the study were that precipitation and water use lead to aboveground primary production, solar radiation and temperature lead to belowground primary production (roots), and temperature and water lead to cool and warm season growth habit. These findings help explain the categories used in Holdridge's bioclassification scheme, which were then later simplified in Whittaker's. The number of classification schemes and the variety of determinants used in those schemes, however, should be taken as a strong indicator that biomes do not all fit perfectly into the classification schemes created.

Holdridge Scheme

The Holdridge classification scheme was developed by L.R. Holdridge, a botanist. It maps climates based on four categories:

- Average total precipitation (cm) on a logarithmic scale.
- Potential evapotranspiration ratio: the potential evapotranspiration divided by the precipitation; the ratio increases from humid to arid regions.
- Potential evapotranspiration
- Mean annual biotemperature (°C): calculated from monthly mean temperatures after converting any mean temperature to 0° C, based on the assumption that temperatures at or below freezing all have the same effect on plants, and delineating between -10° C and -30° C would yield unrealistic results.

In this scheme, climates are classified based on the biological effects of temperature and rainfall on vegetation under the assumption that these two abiotic factors are the largest determinants of the type of vegetation found in an area. Holdridge uses the 4 axis to define 30 so called 'humidity provinces', which are clearly visible in the Holdridge diagram. While the scheme largely ignores soil and sun exposure, Holdridge did acknowledge that these, too, were important factors in biome determination.

Whittaker's Biome-type Classification Scheme

Whittaker appreciated biome-types as a representation of the great diversity of the living world, and saw the need to establish a simple way to classify these biome-types. Whittaker based his classification scheme on two abiotic factors: Precipitation and Temperature. His scheme can be seen as a simplification of Holdridge's, one more readily accessible, but perhaps missing the greater specificity that Holdrige's provides.

Whittaker based his representation of global biomes on both previous theoretical assertions as well as an ever increasing empirical sampling of global ecosystems. Whittaker was in a unique position to make such a holistic assertion as he had previously compiled a review of biome classification.

The Whittaker Classification Scheme can be viewed at the following address:

Key definitions for understanding Whittaker's Scheme

- *Physiognomy*: The apparent characteristics, outward features, or appearance of ecological communities or species.
- *Biome*: a grouping terrestrial ecosystems on a given continent that are similar in vegetation structure, physiognomy, features of the environment and characteristics of their animal communities.
- *Formation*: a major kind of community of plants on a given continent.
- *Biome-type*: grouping of convergent biomes or formations of different continents; defined by physiognomy.
- *Formation-type*: grouping of convergent formations.

Whittaker's distinction between biome and formation can be simplified: formation is used when applied to plant communities only, while biome is used when concerned with both plants and animals. Whittaker's convention of biome-type or formation-type is simply a broader method to categorize similar communities.

Whittaker's Parameters for Classifying Biome-types

Whittaker, seeing the need for a simpler way to express the relationship of community structure to the environment, used what he called 'gradient analysis' of ecocline patterns to relate communities to climate on a worldwide scale. Whittaker considered four main ecoclines in the terrestrial realm.

Intertidal levels: The wetness gradient of areas that are exposed to alternating water and dryness with intensities that vary by location from high to low tide.

- climatic moisture gradient;
- temperature gradient by altitude; and
- temperature gradient by latitude.

Along these gradients, Whittaker noted several trends that allow him to qualitatively establish biome-types.

- The gradient runs from favourable to extreme with corresponding changes in productivity.
- Changes in physiognomic complexity vary with the favorability of the environment (decreasing community structure and reduction of stratal differentiation as the environment becomes less favourable).
- Trends in diversity of structure follow trends in species diversity; alpha and beta species diversities decrease from favourable to extreme environments.
- Each growth-form (i.e. grasses, shrubs, etc.) has its characteristic place of maximum importance along the ecoclines.
- The same growth forms may be dominant in similar environments in widely different parts of the world.

Whittaker summed the effects of gradients (3) and (4), to get an overall temperature gradient and combined this with gradient (2), the moisture gradient, to express the above conclusions in what is known as the Whittaker Classification Scheme. The scheme graphs average annual precipitation (x-axis) versus average annual temperature (y-axis) to classify biome-types.

Humans have fundamentally altered global patterns of biodiversity and ecosystem processes. As a result, vegetation forms predicted by conventional biome systems are rarely observed across most of Earth's land surface. Anthropogenic biomes provide an alternative view of the terrestrial biosphere based on global patterns of sustained direct human interaction with ecosystems, including agriculture, human settlements, urbanization, forestry and other uses of land. Anthropogenic biomes offer a new way forward in ecology and conservation by recognizing the irreversible coupling of human and ecological systems at global scales and moving us toward an understanding how best to live in and manage our biosphere and the anthropogenic biosphere we live in. The main biomes in the world are freshwater, marine, coniferous, deciduous, ice, mountains, boreal, grasslands, tundra, and rainforests.

CHAPTER 17

Coevolution

In a broad sense, biological coevolution is "the change of a biological object triggered by the change of a related object". Coevolution can occur at multiple levels of biology: it can be as microscopic as correlated mutations between amino acids in a protein, or as macroscopic as covarying traits between different species in an environment. Each party in a coevolutionary relationship exerts selective pressures on the other, thereby affecting each others' evolution. Species-level coevolution includes the evolution of a host species and its parasites (host-parasite coevolution), and examples of mutualism evolving through time. Evolution in response to abiotic factors, such as climate change, is not coevolution (since climate is not alive and does not undergo biological evolution). Evolution in a one-on-one interaction, such as that between predator and prey, host-symbiont or host-parasitic pair, is coevolution. But many cases are less clearcut: a species may evolve in response to a number of other species, each of which is also evolving in response to a set of species. This situation has been referred to as 'diffuse coevolution'. And, certainly, for many organisms, the biotic (living) environment is the most prominent selective pressure, resulting in evolutionary change.

The concept of coevolution was briefly described by Charles Darwin in *On the Origin of Species*, and developed in detail in *Fertilisation of Orchids*. It is likely that viruses and their hosts may have coevolved in a number of cases.

One model of the coevolution processes was Leigh Van Valen's Red Queen's Hypothesis. Emphasizing the importance of the sexual conflict, Thierry Lodé privileged the role of *antagonist interactions* (notably sexual) in evolution leading to an antagonist coevolution.

Coevolution does not imply mutual dependence. The host of a parasite, or prey of a predator, does not depend on its enemy for survival.

The existence of mitochondria within eukaryote cells is an example of coevolution as the mitochondria has a different DNA sequence than that of the nucleus in the host cell. This concept is described further by the endosymbiotic theory.

Coevolutionary algorithms are also a class of algorithms used for generating artificial life as well as for optimization, game learning and machine learning. Pioneering results in the use of coevolutionary methods were by Daniel Hillis (who coevolved sorting networks) and Karl Sims (who coevolved virtual creatures).

In his book *The Self-organizing Universe*, Erich Jantsch attributed the entire evolution of the cosmos to coevolution.

In astronomy, an emerging theory states that black holes and galaxies develop in an interdependent way analogous to biological coevolution.

Hummingbirds and Ornithophilous Flowers

Hummingbirds and ornithophilous flowers have evolved to form a mutualistic relationship. It is prevalent in the bird's biology as well as in the flower's. Hummingbird flowers have nectar chemistry associated with the bird's diet. Their colour and morphology also coincide with the bird's vision and morphology. The blooming times of these ornithophilous flowers have also been found to coincide with hummingbirds' breeding seasons.

Flowers have converged to take advantage of similar birds. Flowers compete for pollinators and adaptations reduce deleterious effects of this competition. Bird-pollinated flowers usually show higher nectar volumes and sugar production. This reflects high energy requirements of the birds. Energetic criteria are the most important determinants of flower choice by birds. Following their respective breeding seasons, several species of hummingbirds co-occur in North America, and several hummingbird flowers bloom simultaneously in these habitats. These flowers seem to have converged to a common morphology and colour. Different lengths and curvatures of the corolla tubes can affect the efficiency of extraction in hummingbird species in relation to differences in bill morphology. Tubular flowers force a bird to orient its bill in a particular way when probing the flower, especially when the bill and corolla are both curved; this also allows the plant to place pollen on a certain part of the bird's body. This opens the door for a variety of morphological co-adaptations.

An important requisite for attraction is conspicuousness to birds, which reflects the properties of avian vision and habitat features. Birds have their greatest spectral sensitivity and finest hue discrimination at the long wavelength end of the visual spectrum. This is why red is so conspicuous to birds. Hummingbirds may also be able to see ultraviolet 'colours'. The prevalence of ultraviolet patterns and nectar guides in nectar-poor entomophilous flowers allows the bird to avoid these flowers on sight. Two subfamilies in the family Trochilidae are Phaethorninae and Trochlinae. Each of these groups has evolved in conjunction with a particular set of flowers. Most Phaethorninae species are associated with large monocotyledonous herbs, and members of the subfamily Trochilinae are associated with dicotyledonous plant species.

Angracoid Orchids and African Moths

Another example of coevolution is pollination of Angraecoid orchids by African moths. These species coevolve because the moths are dependent on the flowers for nectar and the flowers are dependent on the moths to spread pollen so they can reproduce. The evolutionary process has led to deep flowers and moths with long probosci.

Old World Swallowtail and Fringed Rue

An example of *Antagonistic Coevolution* is the Old World Swallowtail (Papilio machaon) caterpillar which lives on Fringed Rue (Ruta chalepensis) plant. Rue plant produces etheric oils which repel plant-eating insects. The Old World Swallowtail caterpillar developed resistance to these poisonous substances, thus reducing competition of other plant-eating insects.

Old World Swallowtail (Papilio machaon) caterpillar on Fringed Rue (Ruta chalepensis) plant.

Garter Snake and Rough-skinned Newt

Coevolution can occur between predator and prey species as in the case of the Rough-skinned Newt (*Taricha granulosa*) and the common garter snake (*Thamnophis sirtalis*). In this case, the newts produce a potent nerve toxin that concentrates in their skin. Garter snakes have evolved resistance to this toxin through a set of genetic mutations, and prey upon the newts. The relationship between these animals has resulted in an evolutionary arms race that has driven toxin levels in the newt to extreme levels. This is an example of co-evolution because both organisms changed to better increase their chance of survival.

California Buckeye and Pollinators

When bee-hives are kept whose bee species that have not coevolved with the California Buckeye, toxicity to aesculin, a neurotoxin present in the flower nectar of the *Aesculus californica* tree may be noted; this toxicity is only thought to be present in the case of honeybees and other insecta, which species did not coevolve with A. californica.

Acacia Ant and Swollen Thorn Acacia Tree

The ant provides protection for the tree against preying insects and other plants competing for sunlight, and the tree provides nourishment and shelter for the ant and the ants' larvae.

Technological Coevolution

Computer software and hardware can be considered as two separate components but tied intrinsically by coevolution. Similarly, operating systems and computer applications, web browsers and web applications. All of these systems depend upon each other and advance step by step through a kind of evolutionary process. Changes in hardware, an operating system or web browser may introduce new features that are then incorporated into the corresponding applications running alongside.

Mutualism (Biology)

Mutualism is the way two organisms biologically interact where each individual derives a fitness benefit (i.e. increased survivorship). Similar interactions within a species are known as co-operation. It can be contrasted with interspecific competition, in which each species experiences *reduced* fitness, and exploitation, or parasitism, in which one species benefits at the *expense* of the other. Mutualism and symbiosis are sometimes used as if they are synonymous, but this is strictly incorrect: symbiosis is a broad category, defined to include relationships which are mutualistic, parasitic or commensal. Mutualism is only one *type*.

A well known example of mutualism is the relationship between ungulates (such as cows) and bacteria within their intestines. The ungulates benefit from the cellulase produced by the bacteria, which facilitates digestion; the bacteria benefit from having a stable supply of nutrients in the host environment.

Mutualism plays a key part in ecology. For example, mutualistic interactions are vital for terrestrial ecosystem function as more than 70 per cent of land plants rely on mycorrhizal relationships with fungi to provide them with inorganic compounds and trace elements.

In addition, mutualism is thought to have driven the evolution of much of the biological diversity we see, such as flower forms (important for pollination mutualisms) and co-evolution between groups of species. However mutualism has historically received less attention than other interactions such as predation and parasitism.

Measuring the exact fitness benefit to the individuals is not always straightforward, particularly when the individuals can receive benefits from a range of species, for example most plant-pollinator mutualisms. It is therefore common to categorise mutualisms according to the closeness of the association, using terms such as obligate versus facultative. Defining 'closeness', however, is also problematic. It can refer to mutual dependency (the species cannot live without one another) or the biological intimacy of the relationship in relation to physical closeness (e.g. one species living within the tissues of the other species).

Resource-resource Relationships

Resource-resource interactions, in which one type of resource is traded for a different resource, are probably the most common form of mutualism; for example mycorrhizal associations between plant roots and fungi, with the plant providing carbohydrates to the fungus in return for primarily phosphate but also nitrogenous compounds. Other examples include rhizobia bacteria which fix nitrogen for leguminous plants (family Fabaceae) in return for energy-containing carbohydrates.

Service-resource Relationships

Pollination in which nectar or pollen (food resources) are traded for pollen dispersal (a service) or ant protection of aphids, where the aphids trade sugar-rich honeydew (a by-product of their mode of feeding on plant sap) in return for defense against predators such as ladybird beetles.

Phagophiles feed (resource) on ectoparasites, thereby providing anti-pest service.

Zoochory is an example where animals disperse the seeds of plants. This is similar to pollination in that the plant produces food resources (for example, fleshy fruit, overabundance of seeds) for animals that disperse the seeds (service).

Strict service-service interactions are very rare, for reasons that are far from clear. One example is the relationship between sea anemones and anemonefish in the family Pomacentridae: the anemones provide the fish with protection from predators (which cannot tolerate the stings of the anemone's tentacles) and the fish defend the anemones against butterflyfish (family Chaetodontidae) which eat anemones. However, in common with many mutualisms, there is more than one aspect to it: in the anemonefish-anemone mutualism, waste ammonia from the fish feed the symbiotic algae that are found in the anemone's tentacles. Therefore what appears to be a service-service mutualism in fact has a service-resource component. A second example is that of the relationship between some ants in the genus

Pseudomyrmex and trees in the genus *Acacia*, such as the Whistling Thorn and Bullhorn Acacia. The ants nest inside the plant's thorns. In exchange for shelter, the ants protect acacias from attack by herbivores (which they frequently eat, introducing a resource component to this service-service relationship) and competition from other plants by trimming back vegetation that would shade the acacia. In addition, another service-resource component is present, as the ants regularly feed on lipid-rich food-bodies called Beltian bodies that are on the *Acacia* plant.

In the Neotropics, the ant, *Myrmelachista schumanni* makes its nest in special cavities in *Duroia hirsute*. Plants in the vicinity which belong to other species are killed with formic acid. This selective gardening can be so aggressive that small areas of the rainforest are dominated by *Duroia hirsute*. These peculiar patches are known by local people as 'devil's gardens'.

In some of these relationships, the cost of the ant's protection can be quite expensive. *Cordia* sp. trees in the Amazonian rainforest have a kind of partnership with *Allomerus* sp. ants, which make their nests in modified leaves. To increase the amount of living space available, the ants will destroy the tree's flower buds. The flowers die and leaves develop instead, provisioning the ants with more dwellings. Another type of *Allomerus* sp. ant lives with the *Hirtella* sp. tree in the same forests, but in this relationship the tree has turned the tables on the greedy ants. When the tree is ready to produce flowers, the ant abodes on certain branches begin to wither and shrink, forcing the occupants to flee, leaving the tree's flowers to develop free from ant attack.

Humans also engage in mutualisms with other species, including their gut flora (without which they would not be able to digest food efficiently) and domesticated animals such as horses, which provide transportation in return for food and shelter. In traditional agriculture, many plants will function mutualistically as companion plants, providing each other with shelter, soil fertility and the repelling of pests. For example, beans may grow up cornstalks as a trellis, while fixing nitrogen in the soil for the corn, as exploited in the Three Sisters gardening technique.

Mutualism is essentially the logistic growth equation + mutualistic interaction. The mutualistic interaction term represents the increase in population growth of species one as a result of the presence of greater numbers of species two, and vice versa. Wright also considered the concept of saturation, which means that with higher densities, there are decreasing benefits of further increases of the mutualist population. Without saturation, species' densities would increase indefinitely. Because that isn't possible due to environmental constraints and carrying capacity, a model that includes saturation would be more accurate. Wright's mathematical theory is based on the premise of a simple two-species mutualism model in which the benefits of mutualism become saturated due to limits posed by handling time. Wright defines handling time as the time needed to process a food item, from the initial interaction to the start of a search for new food items and assumes that processing of food and searching for food are mutually exclusive. Mutualists that display foraging behaviour are exposed to the restrictions on handling time. Mutualism can be associated with symbiosis.

CHAPTER 18

Biological Interaction

Biological interactions result from the fact that organisms in a community interact with each other. In the natural world, no organism is an autonomous entity isolated from its surroundings. It is part of its environment, rich in living and non-living elements, all of which interact with each other in some fashion. An organism's interactions with its environment are fundamental to the survival of that organism and the functioning of the ecosystem as a whole.

Primary Succession is a series of changes that occur in an area where no soil or organisms live. Secondary Succession is a series of changes occurring in an area where the ecosystems been disturbed, but soil and organisms are still existing.

In ecology, biological interactions are the relationships between two species in an ecosystem. These relationships can be categorized into many different classes of interactions based either on the effects or on the mechanism of the interaction. The interactions between two species vary greatly in these aspects as well as in duration and strength. Species may meet once in a generation (e.g. pollination) or live completely within another (e.g. endosymbiosis). Effects may range from one species eating the other (predation), to mutual benefit (mutualism). The interactions between two species need not be through direct contact. Due to the connected nature of ecosystems, species may affect each other through intermediaries such as shared resources or common enemies.

Terms which explicitly indicate the quality of benefit or harm in terms of fitness experienced by participants in an interaction are listed below. There are six possible combinations, ranging from mutually beneficial through neutral to mutually harmful interactions. The level of benefit or harm is continuous and not discrete, such that an interaction may be trivially harmful through to deadly, for example. It is important to note that these interactions are not always static. In many cases, two species will interact differently under different conditions. This is particularly true in, but not limited to, cases where species have multiple, drastically different life stages.

Neutralism

Neutralism describes the relationship between two species which interact but do not affect each other. It describes interactions where the fitness of one species has absolutely no effect whatsoever on that of the other. True neutralism is extremely unlikely or even impossible to prove. When dealing with the complex networks of interactions presented by ecosystems, one cannot assert positively that there is absolutely no competition between or benefit to either species. Since true neutralism is rare or non-existent, its usage is often extended to situations where interactions are merely insignificant or negligible.

Amensalism

Amensalism between two species involves one impeding or restricting the success of the other while the other species has no effect on it. It is a type of symbiosis. Usually this occurs when one organism exudes a chemical compound as part of its normal metabolism that is detrimental to another organism.

The bread mold Penicillium is a common example of this; penicillium secrete penicillin, a chemical that kills bacteria. A second example is the black walnut tree (*Juglans nigra*), which secrete juglone, a chemical that harms or kills some species of neighbouring plants, from its roots. This interaction may still increase the fitness of the non-harmed organism though, by removing competition and allowing it access to greater scarce resources. In this sense the impeding organism can be said to be negatively affected by the other's very existence, making it a +/- interaction. A third simple example is when sheep or cattle make trails in grass that they trample on, and without realizing, they are killing the grass.

Competition

Competition is a mutually detrimental interaction between individuals, populations or species, but rarely between clades.

Synnecrosis is a particular case in which the interaction is so mutually detrimental that it results in death, as in the case of some parasitic relationships. It is a rare and necessarily short-lived condition as evolution selects against it. The term is seldom used.

Competition can be defined as an interaction between organisms or species, in which the fitness of one is lowered by the presence of another.

Limited supply of at least one resource (such as food, water, and territory) used by both is required. Competition is one of many interacting biotic and abiotic factors that affect community structure. Competition among members of the same species is known as intraspecific competition, while competition between individuals of different species is known as interspecific competition. Though intraspecific competition has been well documents the validity of interspecific competition, especially among large groups has been debated. Competition is not always a straightforward, direct interaction either, and can occur in both a direct and indirect fashion.

According to the competitive exclusion principle, species less suited to compete for resources should either adapt or die out. According to evolutionary theory, this competition within and between species for resources plays a critical role in natural selection.

Antagonism

In antagonistic interactions one species benefits at the expense of another. Predation is an interaction between organisms in which one organism captures biomass from another. It is often used as a synonym for carnivory but in its widest definition includes all forms of one organism eating another, regardless of trophic level (e.g. herbivory), closeness of association (e.g. parasitism and parasitoidism) and harm done to prey (e.g. grazing). Other interactions that cannot be classed as predation however are still possible, such as Batesian mimicry, where an organism bears a superficial similarity of at least one sort, such as a harmless plant coming to mimic a poisonous one.

Ecological Facilitation

The following two interactions can be classed as facilitative. *Facilitation* describes species interactions that benefit at least one of the participants and cause no harm to either. Facilitations can be categorized as mutualisms, in which both species benefit, or commensalisms, in which one species benefits and the other is unaffected. Much of classic ecological theory (e.g., natural selection, niche separation, metapopulation dynamics) has focussed on negative interactions such as predation and competition, but positive interactions (facilitation) are receiving increasing focus in ecological research.

Commensalism

Commensalism benefits one organism and the other organism is neither benefited nor harmed. It occurs when one organism takes benefits by interacting with another organism by which the host organism is not affected. A good example is a remora living with a shark. Remoras eat leftover food from the shark. The shark is not affected in the process as remoras eat only leftover food of the shark which doesn't deplete the sharks resources.

The term symbiosis (Greek: living together) can be used to describe various degrees of close relationship between organisms of different species. Sometimes it is used only for cases where both organisms benefit, sometimes it is used more generally to describe all varieties of relatively tight relationships, i.e. even parasitism, but not predation. Some even go so far as to use it to describe predation. It can be used to describe relationships where one organism lives on or in another, or it can be used to describe cases where organisms are related by mutual stereotypic behaviours.

In either case symbiosis is much more common in the living world and much more important than is generally assumed. Almost every organism has many internal parasites. A large percentage of herbivores have mutualistic gut fauna that help them digest plant matter, which is more difficult to digest than animal prey. Coral reefs are the result of mutalisms between coral organisms and various types of algae that live inside them. Most land plants and thus, one might say, the very existence of land ecosystems rely on mutualisms between the plants which fix carbon from the air, and Mycorrhyzal fungi which help in extracting minerals from the ground. The evolution of all eukaryotes (plants, animals, fungi, protists) is believed to have resulted from a symbiosis between various sorts of bacteria: endosymbiotic theory.

CHAPTER 19

Ecological Stability

Ecological stability can refer to types of stability in a continuum ranging from resilience (returning quickly to a previous state) to constancy to persistence. The precise definition depends on the ecosystem in question, the variable or variables of interest, and the overall context. In the context of conservation ecology, stable populations are often defined as ones that do not go extinct. Researchers applying mathematical models from system dynamics usually use Lyapunov stability.

Types of Ecological Stability

Local stability indicates that a system is stable over small short-lived disturbances, while global stability indicates a system highly resistant to change in species composition and/or food web dynamics.

Constancy and Persistence

Observational studies of ecosystems use constancy to describe living systems that can remain unchanged.

Resistance and Inertia (Persistence)

Resistance and *inertia* deal with a system's inherent response to some perturbation.

A perturbation is any externally imposed change in conditions, usually happening in a short time period. Resistance is a measure of how little the variable of interest changes in response to external pressures. Inertia (or persistence) implies that the living system is able to resist external fluctuations. In the context of changing ecosystems in post-glacial North America, E.C. Pielou remarked at the outset of her overview.

"It obviously takes considerable time for mature vegetation to become established on newly exposed ice scoured rocks or glacial till...it also takes considerable time for whole ecosystems to change, with their numerous interdependent plant species, the habitats these create, and the animals that live in the habitats. Therefore, climatically caused fluctuations in ecological communities are a damped, smoothed-out version of the climatic fluctuations that cause them".

Resilience, Elasticity and Amplitude

Resilience is the tendency of a system to return to a previous state after a perturbation. *Elasticity* and *amplitude* are measures of resilience. Elasticity is the speed with which a system returns. Amplitude is a measure of how far a system can be moved from the previous state and still return. Ecology borrows the idea of neighbourhood stability and a domain of attraction from dynamical systems theory.

Conservation Biology

Conservation biology is the scientific study of the nature and status of Earth's biodiversity with the aim of protecting species, their habitats, and ecosystems from excessive rates of extinction. It is an interdisciplinary subject drawing on sciences, economics, and the practice of natural resource management.

The term *conservation biology* was introduced as the title of a conference held at the University of California in La Jolla, California in 1978 organized by biologists Bruce Wilcox and Michael Soulé. The meeting was prompted by the concern among scientists over tropical deforestation, disappearing species, eroding genetic diversity within species. The conference and proceedings that resulted sought to bridge a gap existing at the time between theory in ecology and population biology on the one hand and conservation policy and practice on the other. Conservation biology and the concept of biological diversity (biodiversity) emerged together, helping crystallize the modern era of conservation science and policy.

Description

The rapid decline of established biological systems around the world means that conservation biology is often referred to as a 'Discipline with a deadline'. Conservation biology is tied closely to ecology in researching the dispersal, migration, demographics, effective population size, inbreeding depression, and minimum population viability of rare or endangered species . Conservation biology is concerned with phenomena that affect the maintenance, loss, and restoration of biodiversity and the science of sustaining evolutionary processes that engender genetic, population, species, and ecosystem diversity. The concern stems from estimates suggesting that up to 50 per cent of all species on the planet will disappear within the next 50 years, which has contributed to poverty, starvation, and will reset the course of evolution on this planet.

Conservation biologists research and educate on the trends and process of biodiversity loss, species extinctions, and the negative affect this is having on our capabilities to sustain the well-being of human society. Conservation biologists work in the field and office, in government, universities, non-profit organizations and industry. They are funded to research, monitor, and catalog every angle of the earth and its relation to society. The topics are diverse, because this is an interdisciplinary network with professional alliances in the biological as well as social sciences. Those dedicated to the cause and profession advocate for a global response to the current biodiversity crisis based on morals, ethics, and scientific reason. Organizations and citizens are responding to the biodiversity crisis through conservation action plans that direct research, monitoring, and education programmes that engage concerns at local through global scales.

Context and Trends

Conservation biologists study trends and process from the paleontological past to the ecological present as they gain an understanding of the context related to species extinction. It is generally accepted that there have been five major global mass extinctions that register in Earth's history. These include: the Ordovician (440 mya), Devonian (370 mya), Permian–Triassic (245 mya), Triassic–Jurassic (200 mya), and Cretaceous (65 mya) extinction spasms. Within the last 10,000 years, human influence over the Earth's ecosystems has been so extensive that scientists have difficulty estimating the number of species lost; that is to say the rates of deforestation, reef destruction, wetland draining and other human acts are proceeding much faster than human assessment of species. The latest *Living Planet Report* by the World Wide Fund for Nature estimates that we have exceeded the bio-regenerative capacity of the planet, requiring 1.5 Earths to support the demands placed on our natural resources.

Conservation biologists are dealing with and have published evidence from all corners of the planet indicating that humanity may be living the sixth and greatest planetary extinction event. It has been suggested that we are living in an era of unprecedented numbers of species extinctions, also known as the Holocene extinction event. The global extinction rate may be approximately 100,000 times higher than the natural background extinction rate. It is estimated that two-thirds of all mammal genera and one-half of all mammal species weighing at least 44 kilograms (97 lb) have gone extinct in the last 50,000 years. It is speculated that this sixth extinction period is unique because it would be the first major extinction to be caused by another biotic agent over the course of the Earth's 4 billion year history. The Global Amphibian Assessment reports that amphibians are declining on a global scale faster than any other vertebrate group, with over 32 per cent of all surviving species being threatened with extinction. The surviving populations are in continual decline in 43 per cent of those that are threatened. Since the mid-1980s the actual rates of extinction have exceeded 211 times rates measured from the fossil record. However, "The current amphibian extinction rate may range from 25,039 to 45,474 times the background extinction rate for amphibians." The global extinction trend occurs in every major vertebrate group that is being monitored. For example, 23 per cent of all mammals and 12 per cent of all birds are Red Listed by the International Union for Conservation of Nature (IUCN), meaning they too are threatened with extinction.

Status of Oceans and Reefs

Global assessments of coral reefs of the world continue to report drastic and rapid rates of decline. By 2000, 27 per cent of the world's coral reef ecosystems had effectively collapsed. The largest period of decline occurred in a dramatic 'bleaching' event in 1998, where approximately 16 per cent of all the coral reefs in the world disappeared in less than a year. *Coral bleaching* is caused by a mixture of environmental stresses, including increases in ocean temperatures and acidity, causing both the release of symbiotic algae and death of corals. Decline and extinction risk in coral reef biodiversity has risen dramatically in the past ten years. The loss of coral reefs, which are predicted to go extinct in the next century, will have huge economic impacts, threatens the balance of global biodiversity, and endangers food security for hundreds of millions of people. Conservation biology plays an important role in international agreements covering the world's oceans (and other issues pertaining to biodiversity, e.g.)

> These predictions will undoubtedly appear extreme, but it is difficult to imagine how such changes will not come to pass without fundamental changes in human behaviour.
>
> —*J.B. Jackson*

The oceans are threatened by acidification due to an increase in CO_2 levels. This is a most serious threat to societies relying heavily upon oceanic natural resources. A concern is that the majority of all marine species will not be able to evolve or acclimate in response to the changes in the ocean chemistry.

The prospects of averting mass extinction seems unlikely when "90 per cent of all of the large (average approximately =50 kg), open ocean tuna, billfishes, and sharks in the ocean" are reportedly gone. Given the scientific review of current trends, the ocean is predicted to have few surviving multi-cellular organisms with only microbes left to dominate marine ecosystems.

Insects and Other Groups

There are serious concerns also being hailed from taxonomic groups that do not receive the same degree of social attention or attract funds as the vertebrates do, including fungi, lichen, plant and insect communities where the vast majority of biodiversity is represented. Insect conservation, in particular, is of pivotal importance for conservation biology. The value of insects in the biosphere is enormous because they outnumber all other living groups in measure of species richness. The greatest bulk of biomass on land is found in plants, which is sustained by insect relations. This great ecological value of insects is countered by a society that oftentimes reacts negatively toward these aesthetically 'unpleasant' creatures.

One area of concern in the insect world that has caught the public eye is the mysterious case of missing honey bees (*Apis mellifera*). Honey bees provide an indispensable ecological services through their acts of pollination supporting a huge variety of agriculture crops. The sudden disappearance of bees leaving empty hives or colony collapse disorder (CCD) is not uncommon. However, in 16-month period from 2006 through 2007, 29 per cent of 577 beekeepers across the United States reported CCD losses in up to 76 per cent of their colonies. This sudden demographic loss in bee numbers is placing a strain on the agricultural sector. The cause behind the massive declines is puzzling scientists. Pests, pesticides, and global warming are all being considered as possible causes.

Another highlight that links conservation biology to insects, forests, and climate change is the mountain pine beetle (*Dendroctonus ponderosae*) epidemic of British Columbia, Canada, which has infested 470,000 km^2 (180,000 sq mi) of forested land since 1999. An action plan has been prepared by the Government of British Columbia to address this problem.

> This impact converted the forest from a small net carbon sink to a large net carbon source both during and immediately after the outbreak. In the worst year, the impacts resulting from the beetle outbreak in British Columbia were equivalent to 75 per cent of the average annual direct forest fire emissions from all of Canada during 1959-1999.
>
> —Kurz *et al.*

Conservation Biology of Parasites

A large proportion of parasite species are threatened by extinction. A few of them are being eradicated as pests of humans or domestic animals, however, most of them are harmless. Threats include the decline or fragmentation of host populations, or the extinction of host species.

Threats to Biodiversity

Many of the threats to biodiversity, including disease and climate change, are reaching inside borders of protected areas, leaving them 'not-so protected' (e.g. Yellowstone National Park). Climate change, for example, is often cited as a serious threat in this regard, because there is a feedback loop between species extinction and the release of carbon dioxide into the atmosphere. Ecosystems store and cycle large amounts of carbon to regulate global conditions. The effects of global warming adds a catastrophic threat toward a mass extinction of global biological diversity. The extinction threat is estimated to range from 15 to 37 per cent of all species by 2050, or 50 per cent of all species over the next 50 years.

Some of the most significant and insidious threats to biodiversity and ecosystem processes include climate change, mass agriculture, deforestation, overgrazing, slash-and-burn agriculture, urban development, wildlife trade, light pollution and pesticide use. Habitat fragmentation poses one of the more difficult challenges, because the global network of protected areas only covers 11.5 per cent of the Earth's surface. A significant consequence of fragmentation and lack of linked protected areas is the reduction of animal migration on a global scale. Considering that billions of tonnes of biomass are responsible for nutrient cycling across the earth, the reduction of migration is a serious matter for conservation biology.

Human activities are associated directly or indirectly with nearly every aspect of the current extinction spasm.

Wake and Vredenburg

These figures do not imply, however, that human activities must necessarily cause irreparable harm to the biosphere. With conservation management and planning for biodiversity at all levels, from genes to ecosystems, there are examples where humans mutually coexist in a sustainable way with nature. However, it may be too late for human intervention to reverse the current mass extinction.

Extinction rates are measured in a variety of ways. Conservation biologists measure and apply statistical measures of fossil records, rates of habitat loss, and a multitude of other variables such as loss of biodiversity as a function of the rate of habitat loss and site occupancy to obtain such estimates. The Theory of Island Biogeography is possibly the most significant contribution toward the scientific understanding of both the process and how to measure the rate of species extinction. The current background extinction rate is estimated to be one species every few years.

The measure of ongoing species loss is made more complex by the fact that most of the Earth's species have not been described or evaluated. Estimates vary greatly on how many species actually exist (estimated range: 3,600,000-111,700,000) to how many have received a species binomial (estimated range: 1.5-8 million). Less than one per cent of all species that have been described have been studied beyond simply noting its existence. From these figures, the IUCN reports that 23 per cent of vertebrates, 5 per cent of invertebrates and 70 per cent of plants that have been evaluated are designated as endangered or threatened.

Systematic Conservation Planning

Systematic conservation planning is an effective way to seek and identify efficient and effective types of reserve design to capture or sustain the highest priority biodiversity values and to work with communities in support of local ecosystems. Margules and Pressey identify six interlinked stages in the systematic planning approach:

- Compile data on the biodiversity of the planning region
- Identify conservation goals for the planning region
- Review existing conservation areas
- Select additional conservation areas
- Implement conservation actions
- Maintain the required values of conservation areas

Conservation biologists regularly prepare detailed conservation plans for grant proposals or to effectively coordinate their plan of action and to identify best management practices (e.g. Systematic strategies generally employ the services of Geographic Information Systems to assist in the decision making process.

Conservation Biology as a Profession

The Society for Conservation Biology is a global community of conservation professionals dedicated to advancing the science and practice of conserving biodiversity. Conservation biology as a discipline reaches beyond biology, into subjects such as philosophy, law, economics, humanities, arts, anthropology, and education. Within biology, conservation genetics and evolution are immense fields unto themselves, but these disciplines are of prime importance to the practice and profession of conservation biology.

Is conservation biology an objective science when biologists advocate for an inherent value in nature? Do conservationists introduce bias when they support policies using qualitative description, such as habitat *degradation*, or *healthy* ecosystems? As all scientists hold values, so do conservation biologists. Conservation biologists advocate for reasoned and sensible management of natural resources and do so with a disclosed combination of science, reason, logic, and values in their conservation management plans. This sort of advocacy is similar to the medical profession advocating for healthy lifestyle options, both are beneficial to human well-being yet remain scientific in their approach. Many conservation biologists, in addition to having a Bachelors of Science (or extensive natural experience) often receive professional accreditation during their career.

There is a movement in conservation biology suggesting a new form of leadership is needed to mobilize conservation biology into a more effective discipline that is able to communicate the full scope of the problem to society at large. The movement proposes an adaptive leadership approach that parallels an adaptive management approach. The concept is based on a new philosophy or leadership theory steering away from historical notions of power, authority, and dominance. Adaptive conservation leadership is reflective and more equitable as it applies to any member of society who can mobilize others toward meaningful change using communication techniques that are inspiring, purposeful, and collegial. Adaptive conservation leadership and mentoring programmes are being implemented by conservation biologists through organizations such as the Aldo Leopold Leadership Programme.

Approaches

Conservation may be classified as either *in-situ* conservation, which is protecting an endangered species in its natural habitat, or *ex-situ* conservation, which occurs outside the natural habitat. In-situ conservation involves protecting or cleaning up the habitat itself which may include a great deal of environmental preservation, or by defending the species from predators. *Ex-situ* conservation may be used on some or all of the population, when in-situ conservation is too difficult, or impossible.

Also, non-interference may be used, which is termed a preservationist method. Preservationists advocate for giving areas of nature and species a protected existence that halts interference from the humans. In this regard, conservationists differ from preservationists in the social dimension, as conservation biology engages society and seeks equitable solutions for both society and ecosystems.

Some preservationists emphasize the potential of biodiversity in a world without humans:

> "Animals have not yet invaded 2/3 of Earth's habitats, and it could be that without human influence the diversity of tetrapods will continue to increase in an exponential fashion".
>
> —Sahney *et al.*

Ethics and Values

Conservation biologists are interdisciplinary researchers that practice ethics in the biological and social sciences. Chan states that conservationists must advocate for biodiversity and can do so in a scientifically ethical manner by not promoting simultaneous advocacy against other competing values. A conservationist researches biodiversity and reasons through a Resource Conservation Ethic , which identify what measures will deliver "the greatest good for the greatest number of people for the longest time".

Some conservation biologists argue that nature has an intrinsic value that is independent of anthropocentric usefulness or utilitarianism. Intrinsic value advocates that a gene, or species, be valued because they have a utility for the ecosystems they sustain. Aldo Leopold was a classical thinker and writer on such conservation ethics whose philosophy, ethics and writings are still valued and revisited by modern conservation biologists. His writing is oftentimes required reading for those in the profession.

Conservation Priorities

A pie chart image showing the relative biomass representation in a rain forest through a summary of children's perceptions from drawings and artwork, through a scientific estimate of actual biomass, and by a measure of biodiversity. Notice that the biomass of social insects far outweighs the number of species.

While most in the community of conservation science 'stress the importance' of sustaining biodiversity, there is debate on how to prioritize genes, species, or ecosystems, which are all components of biodiversity. While the predominant approach to date has been to focus efforts on endangered species by conserving *biodiversity hotspots,* some scientists (e.g.) and conservation organizations, such as the Nature Conservancy, argue that it is more cost effective, logical, and socially relevant to invest in *biodiversity coldspots*. The costs of discovering, naming, and mapping out the distribution every species, they argue, is an ill advised conservation venture. They reason it is better to understand the significance of the ecological roles of species.

Biodiversity hotspots and coldspots are a way of recognizing that the spatial concentration of genes, species, and ecosystems is not uniformly distributed on the Earth's surface. For example, "44 per cent of all species of vascular plants and 35 per cent of all species in four vertebrate groups are confined to 25 hotspots comprising only 1.4 per cent of the land surface of the Earth".

Those arguing in favour of setting priorities for coldspots point out that there are other measures to consider beyond biodiversity. They point out that emphasizing hotspots downplays the importance of the social and ecological connections to vast areas of the Earth's ecosystems where biomass, not biodiversity, reigns supreme. It is estimated that 36 per cent of the Earth's surface, encompassing 38.9 per cent of the worlds vertebrates, lacks the endemic species to qualify as biodiversity hotspot. Moreover, measures show that maximizing protections for biodiversity does not capture ecosystem services any better than targeting randomly chosen regions. Population level biodiversity (i.e. coldspots) are disappearing at a rate that is ten times that at the species level. The level of importance in addressing biomass versus endemism as a concern for conservation biology is highlighted in literature measuring the level of threat to global ecosystem carbon stocks that do not necessarily reside in areas of endemism. A hotspot priority approach would not invest so heavily in places such as steppes, the Serengeti, the Arctic, or taiga. These areas contribute a great abundance of population (not species) level biodiversity and ecosystem services, including cultural value and planetary nutrient cycling.

Those in favour of the hotspot approach point out that species are irreplaceable components of the global ecosystem, they are concentrated in places that are most threatened, and should therefore receive maximal strategic protections. The IUCN Red List categories, which appear on Wikipedia species articles, is an example of the hotspot conservation approach in action; species that are not rare or endemic are listed the least concern and their wikipedia articles tend to be ranked low on the importance scale. This is a hotspot approach because the priority is set to target species level concerns over population level or biomass. Species richness and genetic biodiversity contributes to and engenders ecosystem stability, ecosystem processes, evolutionary adaptability, and biomass. Both sides agree, however, that conserving biodiversity is necessary to reduce the extinction rate and identify an inherent value in nature; the debate hinges on how to prioritize limited conservation resources in the most cost effective way.

Economic Values and Natural Capital

Conservation biologists have started to collaborate with leading global economists to determine how to measure the wealth and services of nature and to make these values apparent in global market transactions. This system of accounting is called *natural capital* and would, for example, register the value of an ecosystem before it is cleared to make way for development. The

WWF publishes its *Living Planet Report* and provides a global index of biodiversity by monitoring approximately 5,000 populations in 1,686 species of vertebrate (mammals, birds, fish, reptiles, and amphibians) and report on the trends in much the same way that the stock market is tracked.

This method of measuring the global economic benefit of nature has been endorsed by the G8+5 leaders and the European Commission. Nature sustains many ecosystem services that benefit humanity. Many of the earths ecosystem services are public goods without a market and therefore no price or value. When the *stock market* registers a financial crisis, traders on Wall Street are not in the business of trading stocks for much of the planet's living natural capital stored in ecosystems. There is no natural stock market with investment portfolios into sea horses, amphibians, insects, and other creatures that provide a sustainable supply of ecosystem services that are valuable to society. The ecological footprint of society has exceeded the bio-regenerative capacity limits of the planet's ecosystems by about 30 per cent, which is the same percentage of vertebrate populations that have registered decline from 1970 through 2005.

The ecological credit crunch is a global challenge. The Living Planet Report 2008 tells us that more than three quarters of the world's people live in nations that are ecological debtors — their national consumption has outstripped their country's biocapacity. Thus, most of us are propping up our current lifestyles, and our economic growth, by drawing (and increasingly overdrawing) upon the ecological capital of other parts of the world.

The inherent natural economy plays an essential role in sustaining humanity, including the regulation of global atmospheric chemistry, pollinating crops, pest control, cycling soil nutrients, purifying our water supply, supplying medicines and health benefits, and unquantifiable quality of life improvements. There is a relationship, a correlation, between markets and natural capital, and social income inequity and biodiversity loss. This means that there are greater rates of biodiversity loss in places where the inequity of wealth is greatest.

Although a direct market comparison of natural capital is likely insufficient in terms of human value, one measure of ecosystem services suggests the contribution amounts to trillions of dollars yearly. For example, one segment of North American forests has been assigned an annual value of 250 billion dollars; as another example, honey-bee pollination is estimated to provide between 10 and 18 billion dollars of value yearly. The value of ecosystem services on one New Zealand island has been imputed to be as great as the GDP of that region. This planetary wealth is being lost at an incredible rate as the demands of human society is exceeding the bio-regenerative capacity of the Earth. While biodiversity and ecosystems are resilient, the danger of losing them is that humans cannot recreate many ecosystem functions through technological innovation.

STRATEGIC SPECIES CONCEPTS

Keystone Species

Some species, called a *keystone species,* form a central supporting hub in the ecosystem. The loss of such a species results in a collapse in ecosystem function, as well as the loss of coexisting species. The importance of a keystone species was shown by the extinction of the Steller's Sea Cow (*Hydrodamalis gigas*) through its interaction with sea otters, sea urchins, and kelp. Kelp beds grow and form nurseries in shallow waters to shelter creatures that support the food chain. Sea urchins feed on kelp, while sea otters feed on sea urchins. With the rapid decline of sea otters due to overhunting, sea urchin populations grazed unrestricted on the kelp beds and the ecosystem collapsed. Left unchecked, the urchins destroyed the shallow water kelp communities that supported the Steller's Sea Cow's diet and hastened their demise. The sea otter is a keystone species because the coexistence of many ecological associates in the kelp beds relied upon otters for their survival.

Indicator Species

An *indicator species* has a narrow set of ecological requirements, therefore they become useful targets for observing the health of an ecosystem. Some animals, such as amphibians with their semi-permeable skin and linkages to wetlands, have an acute sensitivity to environmental harm and thus may serve as a *miner's canary*. Indicator species are monitored in an effort to capture environmental degradation through pollution or some other link to proximate human activities. Monitoring an indicator species is a measure to determine if there is a significant environmental impact that can serve to advise or modify practice, such as through different forestsilviculture treatments and management scenarios, or to measure the degree of harm that a pesticide may impart on the health of an ecosystem.

Government regulators, consultants, or NGOs regularly monitor indicator species, however, there are limitations coupled with many practical considerations that must be followed for the approach to be effective. It is generally recommended that multiple indicators (genes, populations, species, communities, and landscape) be monitored for effective conservation measurement that prevents harm to the complex, and oftentimes unpredictable, response from ecosystem dynamics.

Umbrella and Flagship Species

An example of an *umbrella species* is the Monarch butterfly, because of its lengthy migrations and aesthetic value. The Monarch migrates across North

America, covering multiple ecosystems and so requires a large area to exist. Any protections afforded to the Monarch butterfly will at the same time umbrella many other species and habitats. An umbrella species is often used as *flagship species*, which are species, such as the Giant Panda, the Blue Whale, the tiger, the mountain gorilla and the Monarch butterfly, that capture the public's attention and attract support for conservation measures.

Efforts to conserve and protect *global* biodiversity are a recent phenomenon. Prior to the global conservation era, there was the coming of the age of conservation. Some historians have linked this with the 1916 National Parks Act, which included the 'use without impairment' clause, sought by John Muir. This eventually resulted in the removal of a proposal to build a dam in Dinosaur National Monument in 1959.

Natural resource conservation, however, has a history that extends prior to the age of conservation. Resource ethics grew out of necessity through direct relations with nature. Regulation or communal restraint became necessary to prevent selfish motives from taking more than could be locally sustained, therefore compromising the long-term supply for the rest of the community. This social dilemma with respect to natural resource management is often called the 'Tragedy of the Commons'. From this principal, conservation biologists can trace communal resource based ethics throughout cultures as a solution to communal resource conflict. For example, the Alaskan Tlingit peoples and the Haida of the Pacific Northwest had resource boundaries, rules, and restrictions among clans with respect to the fishing of Sockeye Salmon. These rules were guided by clan elders who knew life-long details of each river and stream they managed. There are numerous examples in history where cultures have followed rules, rituals, and organized practice with respect to communal natural resource management.

Conservation ethics are also found in early religious and philosophical writings. There are examples in the Tao, Shinto, Hindu, Islamic and Buddhist traditions. In Greek philosophy, Plato lamented about pasture land degradation: "What is left now is, so to say, the skeleton of a body wasted by disease; the rich, soft soil has been carried off and only the bare framework of the district left". In the bible, through Moses, God commanded to let the land rest from cultivation every seventh year. Before the 18th century, however, much of European culture considered it a pagan view to admire nature. Wilderness was denigrated while agricultural development was praised. However, as early as AD 680 a wildlife sanctuary was founded on the Farne Islands by St Cuthbert in response to his religious beliefs.

In the 20th century, actions in the United Kingdom, United States, and Canada emphasized the protection of habitat areas pursuant to visions of such people as John Muir, Theodore Roosevelt, and Aldo Leopold. While the

Canadian nor the United Kingdom governments did not pioneer the creation of National Parks as the United States did in the late 19th century, there were many far-sighted civil servants who were dedicated to wildlife conservation and of notable mention. Some of these historical figures include Charles Gordon Hewitt and James Harkin.

The term *conservation* came into use in the late 19th century and referred to the management, mainly for economic reasons, of such natural resources as timber, fish, game, topsoil, pastureland, and minerals. In addition it referred to the preservation of forests (forestry), wildlife (wildlife refuge), parkland, wilderness, and watersheds. Western Europe was the source of much 19th century progress for conservation biology, particularly the British Empire with the Sea Birds Preservation Act 1869. However, the United States made contributions to this field starting with thinking of Thoreau and taking form with the Forest Act of 1891, John Muir's founding of the Sierra Club in 1892, the founding of the New York Zoological Society in 1895 and establishment of a series of national forests and preserves by Theodore Roosevelt from 1901 to 1909.

Not until the mid-20th century did efforts arise to target individual species for conservation, notably efforts in big cat conservation in South America led by the New York Zoological Society. In the early 20th century the New York Zoological Society was instrumental in developing concepts of establishing preserves for particular species and conducting the necessary conservation studies to determine the suitability of locations that are most appropriate as conservation priorities; the work of Henry Fairfield Osborn Jr., Carl E. Akeley, Archie Carr and Archie Carr III is notable in this era. Akeley for example, having led expeditions to the Virunga Mountains and observed the mountain gorilla in the wild, became convinced that the species and the area were conservation priorities. He was instrumental in persuading Albert I of Belgium to act in defense of the mountain gorilla and establish Albert National Park (since renamed Virunga National Park) in what is now Democratic Republic of Congo.

By the 1970s, led primarily by work in the United States under the Endangered Species Act along with the Species at Risk Act (SARA) of Canada, Biodiversity Action Plans developed in Australia, Sweden, the United Kingdom, hundreds of species specific protection plans ensued. Notably the United Nations acted to conserve sites of outstanding cultural or natural importance to the common heritage of mankind. The programme was adopted by the General Conference of UNESCO in 1972. As of 2006, a total of 830 sites are listed: 644 cultural, 162 natural. The first country to pursue aggressive biological conservation through national legislation was the United States, which passed back to back legislation in the Endangered Species Act (1966) and National Environmental Policy Act (1970), which together injected major funding and protection measures to large scale habitat protection and threatened species research. Other conservation developments, however, have taken hold throughout the world. India, for example, passed the Wildlife Protection Act of 1972.

In 1980 a significant development was the emergence of the urban conservation movement. A local organization was established in Birmingham, UK, a development followed in rapid succession in cities across the UK, then overseas. Although perceived as a grassroots movement, its early development was driven by academic research into urban wildlife. Initially perceived as radical, the movement's view of conservation being inextricably linked with other human activity has now become mainstream in conservation thought. Considerable research effort is now directed at urban conservation biology. The Society for Conservation Biology originated in 1985.

By 1992 most of the countries of the world had become committed to the principles of conservation of biological diversity with the Convention on Biological Diversity; subsequently many countries began programmes of Biodiversity Action Plans to identify and conserve threatened species within their borders, as well as protect associated habitats. The late 1990s saw increasing professionalism in the sector, with the maturing of organisations such as the Institute of Ecology and Environmental Management and the Society for the Environment.

Since 2000 the concept of landscape scale conservation has risen to prominence, with less emphasis being given to single-species or even single-habitat focussed actions. Instead an ecosystem approach is advocated by most mainstream conservationist, although concerns have been expressed by those working to protect some high-profile species.

Ecology has clarified the workings of the biosphere; i.e., the complex interrelationships among humans, other species, and the physical environment. The burgeoning human population and associated agriculture, industry, and the ensuing pollution, have demonstrated how easily ecological relationships can be disrupted.

Index

– x x x –